DISCARD

DATE DUE

THE MEDIA HANDBOOK

A COMPLETE GUIDE TO ADVERTISING MEDIA
SELECTION, PLANNING, RESEARCH, AND BUYING

LEA's COMMUNICATION SERIES

Jennings Bryant and Dolf Zillmann, General Editors

For a complete list of titles in LEA's Communication Series, please contact Lawrence Erlbaum Associates, Publishers at www.erlbaum.com.

THE MEDIA HANDBOOK

A COMPLETE GUIDE TO ADVERTISING MEDIA
SELECTION, PLANNING, RESEARCH, AND BUYING

Third Edition

Helen Katz
Starcom Media Group

2007

LAWRENCE ERLBAUM ASSOCIATES, PUBLISHERS
Mahwah, New Jersey   London

Lawrence Erlbaum Associates, Inc., Publishers
10 Industrial Avenue
Mahwah, New Jersey 07430
www.erlbaum.com

Cover design by Tomai Maridou

Library of Congress Cataloging-in-Publication Data

Katz, Helen E.
The media handbook: a complete guide to advertising media selection, planning, research, and buying / Helen Katz.—3rd ed.
    p. cm.
Includes bibliographical references and index.
ISBN 0-8058-5717-6 (cloth : alk. paper)—ISBN 0-8058-5718-4 (pbk. : alk. paper) 1. Advertising media planning. 2. Mass media and business. 3. Marketing channels. I. Title.

HF5826.5K38 2007
659—dc22   2005057745
                                                  CIP

Dedication
To my daughters, Stephanie, Caroline, and Vanessa.

Contents in Brief

Contents

Preface

Having already written two versions of this book, the need for another revision may at first seem unnecessary, if not greedy. Hadn't I already answered that perennial question of "What do you do in media" sufficiently? With another 3 years behind us, has the answer really changed? In some ways, the media business (and advertising's role within it) has encountered bigger and more significant changes in the past 3 years than it did in the 10 years since the book was first written.

There are three critical changes in how media today are planned, bought, and sold. These can be thought of as the "3 Cs"—consolidation, consumer control (technology-enabled), and communication accountability. Anyone who follows business news knows that the media business seems to find endless ways to consolidate. Just when you think a company like Viacom or WPP cannot possibly get any bigger, it swallows up another player. The desire to dominate a field—driven in part by stockholder demands for ever-higher profits—leads more and more companies down the path of purchasing their competitors to create something bigger and (they hope) better.

Media planning has, for most of those involved with it on a regular basis, been transformed into communications planning as the definition of "media" has expanded to include everything from the Internet to sports stadiums, to elevator or airport TV screens to event sponsorships and promotions. On the buying side, successive waves of ownership consolidation have reduced the number of media owners significantly in most major media forms, leading to the frequent need to negotiate across media types by owner rather than simply buying time or space in specific vehicles. So while account executives still deal with the client, creatives continue to design the message, and consumer researchers are just as busy focusing on what people think, feel, and do, the media folks have a new and challenging role to play.

The goal of this book, however, remains the same. *The Media Handbook* is written as a basic introduction to the media planning-and-buying process. It can help the college student gain a clearer understanding of what media is and how it fits into the overall marketing process, or it can be a useful reference book for people working in the advertising or media industries whose responsibilities sometimes overlap with the media function. The book begins with a look at the larger marketing, advertising and media objectives, followed by an exploration of major media categories (including the emerging ones, such as branded entertainment and viral marketing). The nuts and bolts of planning and buying take up much of the remainder of the text, with a continued focus on how those tactical elements tie back to the strategic aims of the brand and client.

Media terms are defined when they are introduced so that, in the jargon-filled worlds of media acronyms, the reader will start to feel more comfortable in subsequent discussion of GRPs, DMAs, or BDIs. The book also includes numerous examples, mostly of actual national brands in largely fictitious situations, in order to provide a better sense of how media planning and buying work in the real world. Examples of research studies, from both the industry and the academic world, have been added to give readers additional resources to go to for more in-depth information. At the end of the book, a selection of key resources is offered as an appendix for those individuals or companies that wish to find out more about a particular service or system.

Media planning and buying are not, and should not be thought of as, mystical or esoteric. The media function certainly involves a good deal of expertise and intelligent thinking, and also requires a judicious combination of art and science, creativity, and mathematical applications, but it should be fairly easy to understand to anyone involved in the marketing of a product or service. Indeed, it should really be a prerequisite that all those who are trying to sell something, whether it is a widget or an image, should have the basic knowledge of how media planning operates. That is where the message ends up, and if it is placed incorrectly or not seen by the chosen target audience, even the most creative or inspiring ad will be unable to boost sales.

After reading this new edition of *The Media Handbook*, you will be able to answer the question of what is done in media with confidence, clarity, and a fuller understanding of how media fits in to the larger advertising and marketing picture.

—Helen Katz

Acknowledgments

A third edition may seem, in many ways, to require few acknowledgments. Much of the material is still usable. Updating a few facts and statistics would not seem to require much outside help. But, in fact, many of those who inspired me to write the first edition of this *Handbook* continue to provide inspiration and guidance today. Thus, I would like to thank Mike White and David Drake, both of whom worked with me when I was at DDB Worldwide. They taught me to see the big picture and to think creatively. Kevin Killion, my first boss in the industry, remains a valued friend and mentor, and has as much enthusiasm for media and research today as he did in 1989 when I started at DDB. Since the first edition came out, I have had the opportunity to work with several other inspiring people. At Zenith Media in New York, both Wendy Marquardt and Peggy Green helped me learn much about how media planning and buying truly work together. At GM Planworks, I worked with a stellar group of professionals, from Jana O'Brien at the agency to my clients at General Motors, Michael Browner and Betsy Lazar, all of whom taught me much and challenged me to think more closely about how and why consumers use media. Those lessons are continuing at Starcom Mediavest Group, where Kate Sirkin and Jack Klues educate and inspire me.

I remain grateful to my former professors and supporters from the academic world: Kim Rotzoll, Steve Helle, Kent Lancaster, and Bruce Vanden Bergh all helped me become enamored of research. My editor at Lawrence Erlbaum Associates, Linda Bathgate, has been such a pleasure to work with. She has given me all the trust and support an author could ask for.

And this third revision still required the patience and support of my family—my husband, Eric, and daughters, Stephanie, Caroline, and Vanessa. So it is to them that I dedicate this latest effort. They continue to bring joy and happiness into my life.

Introduction

This book is deliberately designed as a *Media Handbook*. It will not tell you every last detail about each individual medium, nor will it go into great depth on nonmedia advertising elements, such as the creative message or the consumer research that goes on behind the scenes. What it will do, however, is give you a complete picture of how media planning, buying, and research work. You will see what each function entails, and how they fit together with each other and within the framework of the marketing mix. You will know enough by the end of this book to be able to create your own media plan, or undertake a print or broadcast buy. Even if you are not directly responsible for either of those tasks, a greater understanding of how media fit in to the marketing picture will help you communicate with those who do such work. Each chapter builds on and works off the preceding ones, although once you have been through them all, it is designed to be very easy for you to refer to specific tasks or concepts at a later date. At the end of each chapter, you will see a checklist of questions that you should ask yourself if you actually have to fulfill the objective of that particular chapter (e.g., setting objectives or evaluating the plan). At the end of the book, you will find a list of additional resources you can turn to for help in media planning, buying, and research.

CHAPTER 1

What Is Media?

It's 7:30 a.m. You wake up and turn on your satellite radio, then click on the Web to catch the latest world news. During breakfast you turn on the television to catch a few minutes of the morning news shows. Before heading off to work you check your e-mail on the Internet. On the subway, you listen to your iPod (commercial free), looking out of the window at a few outdoor billboards along the highway.

In that brief timespan, you have been immersed in the world of media. Very broadly, that world includes radio, Internet, television, newspapers, magazines, and outdoor billboards. Although you selected satellite radio to listen to music, or the Internet to see the latest news, or the television to watch a program, what you also did was receive information through a means of communication, or a *medium*. Given this broad definition, you can see that there are in fact hundreds of different media available, including direct mail, skywriting, coupons, stadium signs, key-rings, and food containers. All of these, and many other media, offer ways of communicating information to an audience. As advertising media professionals, we are interested in looking at the media as a means of conveying a specific kind of information—an *advertising message*—about a product or service to consumers.

The media play a very important role in our lives. Media help fulfill two basic needs: They *inform* and they *entertain*. We turn, for instance, to the media when we want to hear the latest world news or what happened in financial markets. We also look to the media to fill our evenings and weekends with escapist fare to get us out of our everyday, humdrum routine. Television entertains us with movies, dramas, comedies, game shows, and sports. Radio offers us a wide variety of music, talk, and entertainment. We turn to magazines to find out more about our favorite hobbies and interests. News-

1

papers help us keep up with the world around us. And the Internet provides limitless information that you can search through.

The media's informational role is perhaps best illustrated by considering what happens during a national or international crisis, such as the 2001 terrorist attack on the World Trade Center and Pentagon or the southeast Asian tsunami disaster at the end of 2004. On each occasion, millions of people were glued to their television sets, clicking to favorite Web sites, tuned in to their radios, and reading newspapers and magazines for daily in-depth coverage and subsequent follow-up stories.

The media also affect our lives through their entertainment function. Television situation comedies, such as *All in the Family* and *Mary Tyler Moore*, not only reflected what was happening in U.S. society in the 1970s, but also helped to influence attitudes and behaviors concerning the issues of race and equality. Stories appearing in magazines such as *People* or *InStyle* let us know what is happening in other people's lives, both famous and ordinary. In addition, we increasingly take our cell phones everywhere so that we can go online to get the latest sports scores while we relax.

WHAT MEDIA ARE OUT THERE?

Historically, the world of media was broadly divided into two types—print and electronic. *Print media* include magazines and newspapers, whereas *electronic media* cover radio, television, and the Internet. Other media types are not quite so easily categorized. Thus, outdoor billboards are generally defined as a *print* medium and out-of-home options, such as transit ads or stadium signage, are variously classified as nontraditional, alternative, or ambient media. Exhibit 1.1 provides a list of each type.

In today's ever-changing media world, however, these distinctions are fast becoming obsolete. Is a newspaper that is read online in the print or electronic columns? Where does one place cell phones or word of mouth or product placement? What is increasingly distinguishing one media type from another is how much consumer control there is in the medium's use.

EXHIBIT 1.1   Major print and electronic media

Print Media	Electronic Media
Magazines - Consumer, Farm, Business	Television: Broadcast, Cable, Syndication, Spot
Newspapers - National, Local	Radio: Network, Local
Outdoor billboards	Internet
Direct mail	
Yellow Pages	

Magazines and newspapers have always been under their readers' control; after all, they choose what to read. Regular TV, on the other hand, is more passive; the networks decide what programs to air, and when. But now, with technologies like digital video recorders (DVRs), it is viewers who have become the program schedulers, controlling what they want to see, and when. Here in Exhibit 1.2, is how a list of media types might look if divided into those two categories. This is a topic that will reverberate throughout this book, reflecting one of the major changes in how people use media and, therefore, how the advertising media business works.

THE ROLE OF MEDIA IN BUSINESS

It is important to emphasize here that the focus of this book is commercial media. That is, the communications media we will be talking about are not there simply to beautify the landscape or fill up the pages of a newspaper. They are designed to sell products to customers. Of course, there are also media that convey information but are not commercial in intent. *Consumer Reports* is a magazine that does not carry any advertising. Neither does public television (except for sponsorships, which we'll talk about later). The white pages of the telephone directory, web search engines, and airline safety instructions are all informative, yet these are not advertisements in and of themselves (even if they can carry advertisements within them). And books certainly communicate information to readers. Here, however, we shall concentrate on those media that currently accept advertising messages. It is worth emphasizing the word "*currently*." Twenty-five years ago, you did not find commercial messages at supermarkets, schools, doctors' offices, or ski slopes. Today, advertisers can reach people in all of those places. Even novels are not immune. A popular British author wrote Bulgari Jewelers into her fictional story in 2000, and the company paid her. Hasbro paid young, hip preteens to use its Pox videogame and talk about it with their friends to encourage additional sales. Although these ventures

---

EXHIBIT 1.2   Control vs. noncontrol

Controlled Media	Non-Controlled Media
Magazines	Television (other)
Newspapers	Radio
Direct Mail	Outdoor
Yellow Pages	
Television (via DVRs, Video On Demand)	
Internet	

were criticized by the public, that does not mean there will not be other similar attempts in the future. After all, what is true for today may very well change by tomorrow.

The generic term *media* (or *medium* in the singular) means different things to different people. To Joe Smith sitting at home on a Friday evening, the media mean whatever TV shows he watches or magazines he leafs through. For the local Chevy car dealer, the media provide a way to advertise this week's deals on Impalas and Blazers. And the Podunk Electric Utility Company uses the media to remind its customers that they can get free replacement lightbulbs.

Strictly speaking, a *medium* may be defined as a means by which something is accomplished, conveyed, or transferred. This deliberately broad definition means that consumer media would cover everything from handbills passed out in parking lots, to "For Sale" signs taped to lampposts, to the 10-page advertising supplement that fell out of the last copy of *Business Week* you read, to electronic flashing signs in Times Square, to the young hip folk who are "planted" in certain upscale bars to surreptitiously promote certain liquor brands.

HOW THE MEDIA WORLD HAS CHANGED

The media business can be thought of as an ocean. Each media type starts out as a few drops of water (individual newspapers or radio stations). They flourish and grow, and as more drops form, they start to combine together, creating ponds that turn into streams, rivers, and oceans. There is a certain kind of predictability to it. It starts out small, then expands as more companies enter the field. Over time, a handful of these companies start to grow by buying out their competitors and the industry consolidates to the point where only a few extremely large players remain. This cycle has occurred in all but the newest media, from newspapers to radio to magazines to television. Even the Internet, one of the most diverse media forms in terms of its offerings, has seen those consolidate in recent years as popular Web sites get bought out by larger, better funded companies that are often rooted in traditional media. Take, for example, about.com, a very popular Web site for learning more about any topic. It was purchased in 2005 by the New York Times Company, which saw it as a good "fit" for its information-oriented newspaper. In the outdoor industry, there used to be tens, if not hundreds, of locally based companies, each of which focused its efforts on selling ads in a particular city or region. Today, there are just two companies—Viacom and Clear Channel—that are responsible for more than half of all billboards in the United States.

But what does media industry consolidation have to do with advertising? Why does it matter that the TV network NBC (itself owned by the Universal movie studio) also owns the Bravo cable network and the Spanish-language network Telemundo? How is a media plan or buy affected by the fact that the Tribune Company owns WGN-TV, radio stations, and the *Chicago Tribune* newspaper? Well, although consumers are being offered more and more media choices (more radio stations on satellite radio, more online newspapers, more TV shows they want to watch via their Tivos), the advertisers trying to reach them find that they must negotiate with fewer companies selling advertising space or time. This paradox is something to which we return throughout the book.

MEDIA VERSUS COMMUNICATIONS

In the business world, we think of a medium as a way to transfer and convey information about goods or services from the producer to the consumer, who is a potential buyer of that item. There are various ways to accomplish that in business besides using radio, television, or magazines. Product or company publicity, sales brochures, or exhibits can all be useful ways of conveying information to potential buyers. Note that although this book refers to all potential buyers as "consumers," we should really think of them as *us*. One of the biggest dangers in media planning or buying, as we shall learn in chapter 3, is to categorize viewers, listeners, or readers into broad consumer groups (e.g., "Adults 18–49") that make it too easy to forget that, in the infamous words of one of the founders of the advertising industry, David Ogilvy, "that person is your wife."

Although this book is titled the *Media Handbook*, it is increasingly important to think of media in the broadest terms, as communications. Advertising media used to be thought of solely as traditional, or mass. That is, planners and buyers worked with television, radio, magazines, newspapers, and outdoor. Anything beyond that was considered more specialized. Direct mail was handled by one group, event marketing by another, and promotions by a third. Today, most agencies look for integrated ways to make contact with consumers, whether that is paying to display their brand of soap in "*The Apprentice*," sponsoring a blimp flying over a popular baseball field in the summer, or putting the brand's message on coffee cup holders in Starbucks. The goal of these disparate efforts is to surround the target audience with an holistic campaign that presents them with the same message about the brand in various creative ways.

THE ROLE OF MEDIA IN CONSUMERS' LIVES

As our lives grow increasingly busy and demanding, and as technology moves ahead with sophisticated ways to improve our lives, it seems that the media are playing a more important role in what we do, where we go, or how we behave.

As the example at the opening of this chapter suggested, many of us wake up to the sound of the clock radio; we read the newspaper or check the Internet while watching morning television and eating breakfast; and we connect to our offices via e-mail and a wireless PDA. We commute to work either in the car listening to music on regular or satellite radio, or on the bus or train surrounded by posters with advertising messages on them (or listening to an iPod during the commute). At work, we are likely to see a broad array of Internet advertising or e-mail advertising messages, and many of us watch (or videotape) our favorite soap operas at lunchtime. When we get home in the evening, we'll probably turn on the TV to catch the local news, and after dinner we'll forget about our daily worries by watching a few episodes of prime-time TV that we recorded through our DVRs, while catching up with the daily newspaper. Before we go to sleep for the night, we may check some information online, and then we'll probably glance through a couple of magazines while lying in bed.

When you sit down to watch TV and see a commercial that then appears in a magazine or on a Web site you are browsing through, and it is mentioned again in that night's evening newscast because of the tie-in to a local charity event, you generally don't think about the effort that went into coordinating all of those elements. In fact, if the "seams" between them are too obvious, then something probably isn't working right! Whereas you, as a member of the reading, listening, or viewing audience, are interested primarily in the particular program or publication, the medium is interested in you as a potential buyer, offering you up to advertisers who wish to talk to you.

The role of media in conveying information through advertising messages is not something consumers generally consider. Indeed, when they do think about it they are likely to complain about being inundated by commercial messages! Yet, despite the fact that no one has yet proven "how advertising works," businesses continue to believe in its power, as evidenced by the $264 billion spent on advertising in this country in 2004.

HOW MEDIA WORK WITH ADVERTISING

Advertising in the media performs the dual role of informing and entertaining. It informs us of the goods and services that are available for us to purchase and use. And, along the way, it often entertains us with some humorous, witty, or clever use of words and pictures. For example, let's say you have created a new razor blade for young men that has a built-in counter to tell you how many times you've used it. You've shown it to some friends and neighbors, all of whom are convinced that it would be extremely useful to that target group. You have talked to several distributors and manufacturers of razors who have some interest in producing it. Now, however, the question arises of what to do next. How do you inform people you don't know personally about this wonderful new product?

This is where the media can help. You could place an advertisement on TV announcing this brand new razor type. Perhaps you'd take out magazine ads in men's magazines that show the product and explain what it does. You might create a long-form commercial message, or infomercial, that you pay cable networks targeted to men to air at night and on weekends. You'd want to have a Web site for your new product that allows people to purchase online directly from the site. Your message, that "*Razor Sharp is the razor you can count on*," would then be disseminated to an audience of hundreds, or possibly thousands, depending on your location. You might also generate additional publicity by persuading a national or local celebrity to endorse the product, and send out an electronic news release to TV stations and/or men's magazines. Or, perhaps you would decide to send e-mails out to readers of men's magazines who have opted-in (chosen) to receive such messages, offering them a free sample in exchange for their opinion of the product. Whatever form of communication you use, all involve sending a message through a medium of one kind or another.

Again, it is important to keep in mind that we are talking of media in the broadest sense. So in trying to promote your *Razor Sharp* blades, your TV and print ads or Web site can show people what the product looks like and demonstrate how it works. Then, you might sponsor a men's grooming night at the local department store as a public relations effort to heighten awareness of the product and how well it works. You could send out press releases in advance to notify the media of the event and thereby generate additional publicity both for the event and for your razor. You could offer retailers a special deal, such as contributing funds to the ads that they run (an advertising allowance), if they will promote the product in their weekly newspaper ads. You might also arrange for razors to be handed out on college campuses or health clubs so that people can learn more about *Razor Sharp*. By advertising the product in a wide variety of media, each one fulfills a slightly different role, but your overall message—"*Razor Sharp is the razor you can count on*"—is conveyed clearly and consistently.

Media advertising also performs another vital function. It helps offset the cost of the media communication itself to consumers. If we did not have commercials on television, radio, or the Web, then the cost of the informational or educational content would have to come through sponsorships, taxes, or government monies. Public broadcasting in the United States derives most of its income through semi-annual pledge drives, during which viewers and listeners are asked to give money to pay for the services. Government funding provides additional revenues. But even here, more public broadcasting television stations are accepting restricted forms of paid commercials as long as they are image oriented and not hard sell. Indeed, there is even a network available, Public Broadcasting Marketing, to help advertisers place their spots on public TV stations across the country.

TASKS IN MEDIA

The broad field of advertising media can be broken down into four primary tasks:

- Planning how best to use media to convey the advertising message to the target consumer (the *media planner*)
- Buying media space and time for the message (the *media buyer*)
- Selling that space or time to the advertiser (the *media seller*)
- Researching the relationship between consumers, media, and the brands that advertise to them in those media (the *researcher*).

Most large companies handle the media planning and buying functions through an advertising agency. Smaller firms usually handle this task themselves, through their marketing director or public relations coordinator. The role of the planner is to decide where and when the message should be placed, how often, and at what cost. The plan is then implemented by the media buyer, who negotiates with the media providers themselves to agree on the space and time needed and to determine or confirm where the ad will appear. That buyer will, of course, be dealing with the salesperson at the media company, whose job it is to sell as much advertising space or time as possible. Throughout this process, the researcher tries to offer insights into how and why the media impact the consumer's brand decisions.

SUMMARY

The focus of *The Media Handbook* is the role of media in communicating and conveying information about products and services to potential consumers. It is designed to explore this media world in detail, looking at the changing structure of the industry itself, the various types of communication that are available (printed, aural, visual) and how to use these forms in day-to-day business. The aim here is to provide a better understanding of what the media are and how they work. Media can be classified in several ways—print versus electronic, or active versus passive. Within these categories, consumers choose from a wide array of media in their daily lives, turning to them for both information and entertainment. Advertising in the media also helps to offset the costs of production and distribution. Any company that advertises in the media must deal either directly or indirectly with the planning and buying of advertising space or airtime. This handbook will show you how to do this efficiently and successfully.

Media in the Marketing Context

Although this book is designed to take the media specialist through the planning and buying of media, those functions do not occur in a vacuum. Both media and advertising are part of the bigger picture of the world of marketing. The primary goal of marketing is to increase sales and profits. Consider the example from chapter 1, where we were wondering how to market our reusable razor blade, *Razor Sharp*. We considered many elements beyond which media to use. To market any product effectively involves not simply advertising it, but also figuring out how much to charge for it, where to distribute it, and how to manufacture it. In marketing jargon, these four critical elements are known as the "Four Ps": Product, Price, Place (distribution), and Promotion. Although your job as a media specialist does not necessarily involve making the decisions on all of these criteria, it is critical that you have a clear understanding of how they work, and more importantly, how they can impact your media decisions and strategy. This chapter guides you through these four marketing basics.

In order to sell anything you must first have a *product*, or service. You have to decide how much you need to charge for it (the *price*) so that you can make a profit. You must also figure out how and where the product will be made available to people (*place*, or distribution). And last, but not least, you must consider how you will let potential buyers know what you are offering (*promotion*). Within that last category, there are several key channels of communication: advertising, personal selling, sales promotion, direct marketing, event marketing, and publicity. All can be thought of as media, or ways of conveying information to potential buyers. You can see how these elements work in Exhibit 2.1.

Exhibit 2.1   The Marketing Mix

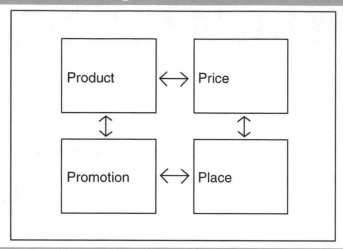

One of the most important things to remember here is that the arrows move in many directions. Almost any decision you make concerning media will have an impact on something else in the marketing mix. For example, if you decided to advertise on network television, then you would have to ensure that your product was in fact available throughout the country. Or, if you chose to concentrate your advertising efforts during holiday periods (Memorial Day, Fourth of July, etc.), then you might consider lowering your price at that time to boost sales even further.

The task of the media planner is to consider all of the marketing information available on the product and use that information to determine how best to reach the target audience with the brand message through advertising media. In this way, the media plan can be thought of as the pivot point, or hub, of the overall marketing plan, as shown in Exhibit 2.2.

Exhibit 2.2   Moving Toward the Media Plan

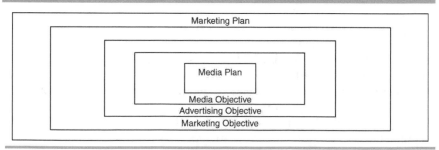

GETTING TO KNOW THE CONSUMER

There are two critical pieces of information that you, as a media specialist, need to know in order to successfully market a product. The first is an understanding of how your consumers view and use your product or service. The second is how they view and use different media types. Although much of the former has been developed over many years and is considered fairly traditional market research, the latter is a relatively new phenomenon within the media world, applying market or consumer research principles and processes to enhance the understanding of how and why people use media. First, this chapter delves into the consumer–brand relationship, and then begins to explore the consumer–media relationship.

Consumers and Brands

First, you must know more about the brand and the product category. A brand is the individual product or service that you are trying to sell. It can be thought of as the name on the label. So Campbell's Tomato soup is a brand, as is their Chicken Noodle soup, or their Clam Chowder variety. The *product category* could either be defined as all brands of tomato soup, or all kinds of soup. In the case of a service, such as insurance, the product category could be one type of insurance (e.g., life, home, or auto) or all types. The brand would be one particular company such as Allstate, or State Farm.

One way to think about brands is to consider your own behavior. When you go to the grocery store, you are usually not thinking in terms of *product categories* or *brands*. More likely, you are thinking about buying a container of Minute Maid orange juice, three Lean Cuisine frozen dinners, or a box of Kellogg's Frosted Flakes cereal. Similarly, when you have to decide which restaurant to go to, you will not categorize them into quick service, family style, or steak houses the way marketers do, but will instead think in terms of the types of food (i.e., Chinese, Mexican, Indian, etc.). And, within those groups, you will probably categorize them by geography, thinking of the specific restaurants by area.

What we need to know as marketers and media specialists, however, is how consumers decide *which* brands and products to buy, as well as the process they go through when purchasing an item. This will vary, depending on the type of product. Whereas a consumer might pick up any brand of floor cleaner, the decision process that person goes through to select a car will take far longer because there are more elements to consider. Understanding these decision processes will help you decide which media might best be used both to reach your target and convey the desired message at the right time. When selling your new razor blade with built-in counter, you could probably use a traditional medium such as magazines to increase awareness of your product. However, a company trying to sell a more complex product (e.g., a car or computer) will likely use a wider variety of communication forms.

Here, we will take a general look at how consumers view and use brands. From there, we can establish some foundations for the media plan. We will do this by going back into the past and looking at what has happened in the marketplace both to the brand and the product category in which we are interested.

In looking at how consumers use brands, we must answer several key questions: How much do consumers already know about the brand (brand and advertising awareness)? And, when, where, and how often do they buy it (purchase dynamics)?

What Do People Know About the Brand?

People have the opportunity to be exposed to at least 5,000 ads every week, so it isn't surprising that they don't remember many of them. In fact, a study conducted by the Newspaper Association of America in the 1990s showed that the percentage of people who can accurately remember the name of the brand they last saw advertised on television had fallen to an all-time low of 4% of those surveyed. Indeed, 86% of TV viewers claim not to attend to regular commercial breaks. And although we talk about "great" ads that we saw on television last night, or perhaps something we read in a newspaper or magazine, we are probably unlikely to remember the brand that was being advertised. Is Tiger Woods the spokesperson for Buick or Chrysler? Does Britney Spears advertise Coca-Cola or Pepsi? In today's increasingly competitive marketing climate, consumers are also likely to be exposed to more than one brand name in an ad. This *comparison advertising* is extremely common in categories such as analgesics, automobiles, and detergents. But although your brand, Brand A, emphasizes how much better it is than Brand B, will your target audience remember A or B?

How the Media Specialist Gets to Know Consumers and Brands

Finding out how aware your consumers are of your brand and its advertising is quite straightforward, although not without pitfalls. The easiest way to do this is through a survey (mail, telephone, or in person) in which you simply ask people what they remember about certain ads. You can do this in one of two ways: *unaided,* where no prompts or assistance are provided; or *aided,* where you offer some kind of memory aid, such as mentioning something from the advertisement or giving an actual list of brand names and asking for further information on the advertising. The unaided method demands more on the part of consumers, asking them to tap deeper into their memories to recall the information you are seeking. With the aided method, you are basically asking people to recognize a brand and/or advertisement when it is placed before them, and then prompting them for additional information about it.[1]

There are other issues to keep in mind with brand-awareness research. The most important is that you cannot expect complete accuracy. That is, there is always the danger with any kind of memory check that you will not get full information from the people you survey. Obviously, the longer the time between when people see an ad and when they are questioned about it, the less they will remember about it. Human memory is highly fallible. They may attribute pieces of one ad to another ad, or recite a list of brand attributes from Brand A that really belong to Brand B. So, if you do test consumer awareness of your ads, be sure to keep in mind the possibility of inaccuracies in the responses.

In addition, you must remember that all of these responses are what consumers *claim* to recognize or recall. Even if you give people a questionnaire to fill out on their own, they may not put down their real feelings or thoughts. They might not want to offend the interviewer or admit how they really feel, or for whatever reason do not want to tell the truth. For instance, they may have only a vague recollection of your brand's name, but they may nevertheless write down that they are very familiar with it.

Having said that, awareness checks do play a vital role in letting you know more about how your consumer interacts with the brand and its advertising. If no one can recall your brand name after it has been advertised on television every day for the past year, then you have a problem. It could be the message isn't convincing at all, or it could be you are advertising it in the wrong medium. Perhaps people can recall the brand name very easily but nothing about the advertising has stuck in their minds.

The goal of increasing brand awareness should not be understated. It is commonly accepted that without consumer awareness of your brand, even the most spectacular media plan will be unlikely to generate many sales. People are far more likely to purchase a brand whose name they have heard before than one about which they have no information. There are many companies that conduct this kind of research. Some of the larger ones are listed in Appendix A.

If you want to probe further into people's responses, then you can find out more through focus groups, which are groups of 5 to 10 people who are interviewed together by a moderator. They are probed for their beliefs, attitudes, or feelings toward a given brand or product category and its advertis-

---

[1]"Recall and Recognition: A Very Close Relationship," Jan Stapel, *Journal of Advertising Research*, vol. 38, no. 4, July/August 1998, 41–46.

ing to help in development of the creative message as well as the marketing and media strategy.

A newer, more in-depth technique for understanding consumers, at least in the marketing world, is the use of *ethnography*. Developed in sociology and anthropology, the technique involves close observation of what consumers are doing. This may include visiting their homes to watch them prepare a meal (for a brand like Kraft salad dressing) or spending a few hours with them in the gym (for a brand like Nike). The idea is to see up close how the brand or product category really fits into people's lives.[2]

The Consumer Decision Process

Many research studies have been conducted over the years to demonstrate the decision process that a consumer typically goes through when buying a routine product. In its simplest form, this process has three steps:

1. Think.
2. Feel.
3. Do.

People must first *think* about the item (i.e., be aware of it and know it exists). They must then develop some kind of attitude or *feeling* toward it (i.e., like it and prefer it to others); and, finally, they must take some action with regard to it (decide on it, and actually buy it). This latter stage is the *do* part of the model.

The process is in fact far more involved than this. We can break these three stages down further, coming up with the following eight stages the consumer goes through in buying a product or service:

1. Need.
2. Awareness.
3. Preference.
4. Search.
5. Selection.
6. Purchase.
7. Use.
8. Satisfaction.

---

[2]See "Consuming Rituals," Lawrence Osborne, *New York Times Magazine,* January 13, 2002, 28–31; "Visual Attention to Programming and Commercials: The Use of In-Home Observations," Dean M. Krugman, Glen T. Cameron, and Candace McKearney White, *Journal of Advertising, vol. 24,* no. 1, Spring 1995, 1–12.

To begin with, consumers must first have a *need* to fulfill. They then become *aware* of the brands available to satisfy that need. After that, several brands are considered acceptable, and a *preference* is developed for one or more of them. The consumer will then *search* for the brand(s) desired, and make a *selection* of one over the others. A specific brand is *purchased* and *used*. Finally, the level of *satisfaction* obtained with that purchase helps determine whether that brand is bought on a future occasion. This is discussed in detail in the next chapter.

Of course, in reality, life isn't always as simple. There are occasions (and products) where people think about a product, buy it, and only at that point do they develop attitudes toward it. This is especially true for new product launches, where consumers have not had a chance to develop emotional bearings for the brand or category. Another point to keep in mind is that the decision process can sometimes get stalled at a point before purchase. In our previous *Razor Sharp* example, your male target may become aware of the brand, decide that he'd like to buy it, and be unable to find it in his grocery store or pharmacy. As a result, he may give up. Or he could try it and then decide he prefers to stick with Gillette's product.

How the Consumer Buys Products

One of the main drawbacks to using surveys or holding discussions with consumers about how they buy is that they are telling you what they *think* they do, which may be very different from what they actually do in real life. Moreover, measuring their brand awareness and advertising recall often ends up being a poor predictor of sales. So, in addition to looking at awareness, or the top of the decision tree, you should also pay attention to what is happening at the bottom of the tree, with the purchase cycle. When are people buying your product? How much is bought? Is there some kind of seasonality to their purchases? All of this information will prove to be critical in planning and buying your media, and it will have a major impact on how and when you schedule your ads.

When Do People Buy?

The answer to this question is more complex than it seems at first. You might say, "Well, they buy my product all the time." But, if you look more closely at purchase behavior, you will probably detect some kind of pattern. People are buying houses "all the time," but they are more likely to do so when interest rates are low and prices are depressed. People buy cars "all the time," but sales increase when the new models come into the showrooms in the fall. In addition, more sales occur in the second half of the month than in the first. Even everyday kinds of items have a timing component to purchases. Sales of cheese are higher on the weekends and around paydays because that is when people have more money to go shopping. Moving companies are busiest between May and October because that is when most people change their residence. Greeting card sales go up before every holiday (whether traditional, e.g., Christmas; or "Hallmark holidays," e.g., Grandparent's Day and Boss' Day).

If you know when consumers are most likely to buy your product, then you can time your media advertising to take advantage of that purchase cycle. For major purchases, in particular, you might also want to consider when people are *thinking about* buying. This might occur several weeks, or even months, before they make the actual purchase. In other words, the Smiths might buy a new Carrier air conditioner in July, but they will probably start to think about which one several months prior to that time. This provides you with a valuable opportunity to get your brand's message to the Smiths early in their decision-making process.

How Much Do They Buy?

The size of consumer purchases is another important element of the purchase cycle with which the media specialist should be familiar. That is, what proportion of your brand's sales comes from each size of the product? For Coca-Cola, it offers numerous sizes of its soda, from 12-ounce cans, to 2-liter bottles, to six-packs. The company needs to know which one is the most popular. Do most people buy their soda in plastic bottles, glass bottles, or cans? Does Coke sell three times as many cans as bottles, perhaps suggesting that this is where the majority of messages should focus? It turns out that nearly 40% of Coca-Cola volume consumed in a 7-day period is in glass bottles, with around 30% each from cans and from plastic bottles (MRI, 2004). This kind of information is not only important for production and distribution purposes, it can also play a key role in your media planning, because the users of each size are likely to be different kinds of people with different media habits. As seen in Exhibit 2.3, the person who chooses to drink glasses of Coca-Cola

EXHIBIT 2.3   Profile of Coca-Cola glass buyer
Male
Precision/Crafts/Repair
Household income $60,000-74,999
Census region: South
A county (urban)
Rent home

Source: MRI 2004

is more likely to be male, with an above-average household income, living in urban areas in the South of the country, and working in precision, craft, or repair jobs, whereas the can drinker is more likely to be a working professional female who is married, college-educated, and living in the north central region of the country. Young working women prefer to watch programs such as "The Simple Life" and "The Bachelorette" and read *Cosmopolitan* and *Glamour;* older adults are more likely to choose "60 Minutes" and *Reader's Digest.* Based on these differences in media preference, you may well end up with two media plans—one for the occasional purchaser of the single can, and another for the frequent user who consumes several plastic bottles per week.

LOOKING AT THE MARKETPLACE

Once you know about how consumers view and use your brand, the next step for the media specialist is to examine what has been happening to that brand in the marketplace in recent times. Given this information on past efforts to sell your product, you can decide whether to continue along the same path or try something different in terms of your media planning and buying. Examining the marketplace involves doing an analysis of historical data on both the brand and the product category. As the famous philosopher George Santayana said, those who do not learn from the past are condemned to repeat it.

Some of the basic questions the media specialist might ask include the following:

- How long has this brand been available?
- How successful has it been throughout its history?
- How has it been positioned in the past?
- What do you know about the company that makes this brand?

You can think of this as genealogical work in that you are trying to dig up as much "family background" on the brand as possible. You may find that the company has been in business for 150 years, suggesting possible leverage to be gained by emphasizing in the message the long heritage the brand possesses and even placing it in media vehicles that have also been around a long time. Or perhaps the company has been around forever, but it is now moving in a different direction and starting to explore new opportunities, suggesting the use of new or different media. Altoids, for example, for many years has made only mints. Recently, it started expanding its product line; first, it created sour candy, then it began moving into the highly competitive chewing gum arena. Despite the fierce competition, the brand captured several market share points because it responded to the underlying consumer desire for a stronger tasting food to eat between meals. But the new product may be targeted at different groups of consumers, which in turn may result in a need for more diverse and/or more selective media. Although its traditional mint brand would continue to have a strong outdoor billboard and print presence to reach a broad audience, the gum would have more appeal to teens and young adults, who might not have seen the ads much before. The company could feature its gum in titles such as *Seventeen* or *Maxim*, appealing to younger people who want to have the latest new products.

WHAT ARE THE COMPETITORS UP TO?

In doing an historical analysis of the brand, you must also deal with competitive issues. That is, you should not only explore and uncover as much marketing and media information as possible about your *own* brand, but you also need to do the same for *all* the brands against which you do or plan to compete. The marketing part of these issues may be divided into three main areas: product category trends, brand trends and share of market, and brand's share of requirements.

Product Category Trends

Whether your brand has been available for half a century, 2 years, or is about to be launched, one of the most important preplanning considerations for the media specialist concerns what is happening in your product category. If you are creating a media plan for the manufacturer of a Cannondale mountain bike, then you would want to know whether sales of bicycles are increasing, decreasing, or flat. That will immediately influence your media budget, who you choose to target, and how you go about trying to reach that group. In some instances, in order to determine how the category has fared, you will have to decide what your "category" really is. If you are selling an oatmeal cookie, then it might seem obvious that it belongs in the cookie category. But perhaps this is a low calorie, low cholesterol cookie that belongs more appropriately in the "diet and health food" classification. Does a yogurt drink fit better into yogurt products or milk drinks? And what about children's software? Does it belong with general software or children's media, such as books and videos?

How you define your product category will determine not only your assessment of the strengths or weaknesses of that category, but also the direction and potential marketing and media strategies you employ for your particular brand. To take the software example, if you decide it is part of the general software category, then you might want to send direct mail to people who have registered their own software and indicated that there are children in the household. If it is classified as a children's product, however, then you will probably do consumer advertising in parenting books such as *Child* magazine. You could also work with schools and libraries to offer special deals offering a free CD if they purchase three titles. Or, you might choose to advertise the product to both target groups using a combination of those media.

There are numerous stories in advertising lore of how the redefinition of a product category gave new life to a moribund product or service. Altoids mints was a small brand with little cachet and low usage. But through unusual advertising focusing on people's desire for a strong-tasting mint that refreshes and even excites, the brand took off. Perhaps the most renowned case of redefinition is that of Arm and Hammer Baking Soda. By finding a new use for an established product (keeping refrigerators smelling fresh), the brand in effect positioned itself in two completely distinct categories—baking products and home fresheners. Today, it has a huge market share in the latter category, and has expanded into numerous other cleanser-related areas, from carpet freshener to toothpaste.

Once you have determined in which product category your brand rightfully belongs (or the category in which you wish it to belong), you are then in a position to examine trends in that category. You can do this in one of several ways. You may have access to product category sales from a trade association or manufacturers' group of some kind (e.g., the Juvenile Products Manufacturers Association, if you are marketing children's toys; or the Electronics Industries Association, if you are marketing electronics items). You can often find such data in trade journals in your particular field (e.g., *Supermarket News* for supermarket food sales or *Chemical Week* for sales of liquid nitrogen). One invaluable source for this type of information is *Sales and Marketing Management,* which comes out several times a year with overall category sales. *Advertising Age* also produces an advertising-to-sales ratio in all major product categories annually that shows spending on advertising relative to sales (see Exhibit 2.4). In many larger companies, these data are routinely collected, usually within the marketing department.

In looking at category trends, be careful to look back beyond the past year. In fact, if you can find 5 to 10 years of data, you'll be in a much stronger position to see the real trends. Another important point to remember is that there will be many factors to explain the rise or fall of product sales. These trends do not occur in a vacuum.

Interpreting Sales Trends. Four factors that help explain sales trends are economic, social, political, and cultural trends. Each will, in turn, influence your media choices. For instance, if you are selling a new high-end plasma TV with lots of fancy features, then the overall health of the economy is going to have a large impact on whether or not people feel they can afford to spend the money on such a piece of entertainment equipment. If you de-

| EXHIBIT 2.4 | Example ad:sales ratio | |

Industry	SIC Code	Advertising as % of sales
Real estate agents and managers	6531	14.0
Amusement parks	7996	9.6
Books: Publishing and printing	2731	7.7
Furniture stores	5712	5.9
Jewelry stores	5944	4.6
Cigarettes	2111	4.0
Eating places	5812	3.2
Women's clothing stores	5621	2.7
Shoe stores	5661	2.4
Poultry slaughter and processing	2015	2.3
Computer communication equipment	3576	2.2
Bakery products 2050	2050	1.2
Grocery stores	5411	1.1
Motion picture theaters	7830	1.0

Source: AdAge.com, 2005

cide that despite the economic downturn you want to emphasize a sophisticated image for your product, aiming it at innovators who always want to buy the latest equipment, then you might use magazines targeted to electronics aficionados, such as *Electronic House* or *Sound & Vision*. If, on the other hand, you choose to emphasize how the large screen returns TV to a family viewing experience, then you might look to a broader audience and use more popular, broad-based vehicles like *FamilyFun* or *Entertainment Weekly*.

Politics can play an important role in the marketing of goods and services. For satellite TV services trying to promote themselves to rival cable subscribers, what happens in Washington at the Federal Communication Commission, or in state or local politics will affect what they are allowed to sell and whether consumers are likely to buy the service. In 1999, satellite TV companies were allowed, for the first time, to beam local channels to their subscribers, a feature that had previously been banned and, therefore, impeded the growth of satellite services. They were quick to advertise this new benefit to prospective customers.

Cultural changes, although slower to occur, can also explain movements in product sales that have implications for media planning and buying. This is seen in the growth of ethnic foods, such as Mexican or Chinese dishes. The increasing popularity of different ethnic food products can be attributed in part to the enormous growth of Hispanic and other immigrant populations in the United States, leading to a greater diversity of cultures that are gradually intermingling and changing tastes and preferences. People living in the West are 17% more likely than the average to consume soy sauce, and 9% less likely than the norm to eat ketchup. The marketers of these foods try different ways of reaching their target audiences, for example, through product sampling in stores or sponsorship of community events.

Finally, social changes, which also tend to happen slowly, can ultimately have a major impact on media activities. The cigarette companies of today have a much tougher job selling their product than they did 20 or 30 years ago, primarily because smoking is no longer considered socially acceptable due to its proven health risks. The marketing task is made more difficult because since 1971 they have been forbidden, by law, from advertising on television at all, and since 1999, from being on any outdoor billboards.

So whereas you, as a media specialist, may not have to pinpoint all the reasons behind category trends, it is important for you to gain a broad understanding of what is really happening in the category and not simply limit yourself to whether sales are up or down. Having this additional background information will help you decide which media you can or should be using in your plan.

What Should You Measure?   Another important issue when looking at category trends is deciding which trends you should be measuring: Sales? Units? Volume? The answer to this may ultimately depend on the types of data you are able to obtain, but you need to keep in mind that what seems to be a trend when examining one number may disappear or be reversed if you turn to another. For example, although sales of your screwdrivers could be going up in dollar terms, you may actually be selling fewer units if sales are rising primarily due to price increases (i.e., you make more money on each unit sold, but sell fewer units as a result). When looking at category trends in dollar terms, always remember to factor in the effects of inflation. What may seem to be a 7% annual growth rate could turn out to be a 2% to 3% rate after accounting for inflation. Perhaps the category trend line shows that the number of units of shampoo sold is declining, but volume is holding steady. This might occur if the unit size has been enlarged, so the same total volume is being sold but in larger bottles. Again, ideally, you want to look at several trend lines using diverse measurements so that you can get an overall picture of what is going on in the category.

Brand Trends

When you turn your attention to individual brands, you perform similar
analyses to those done at the category level. This time, however, you focus
your attention on specific brand names. The use of the plural here is critical: You are not just looking at how *your* brand has been doing over the past
several years, but even more importantly, you need to track how your
brand's *competitors* have been faring during that same period. This requires
finding the answers to the following questions:

- How many competitors are there?
- How many of these are major, and how many minor? In some categories, where there are just a few players (e.g., the airline industry),
you should probably consider all of them, but in larger categories
(e.g., fast food restaurants), where myriad companies have offerings,
you will do better to pay attention to those you believe are your most
serious threats. In certain instances, it is a good idea to look at all of
the competitors regardless of their size; you may find that the
fourth-tier player of 3 years ago has gradually been gaining market
share and is now a far bigger concern. For several years, Dell computers was largely ignored by the likes of IBM and Compaq. Today, however, Dell is the number one seller of personal computers, and IBM no
longer makes them.
- How is the category characterized? Is it an oligopoly, where 3 or 4
brands define the category, or are there 20 or 30 brands each shouting to
be heard?
- How aggressively do the brands in this category compete against
one another? For example, is it advertising driven, or promotion driven,
or does everyone rely heavily on direct mail? You can answer this either
from your own experience in the category, or by looking at any available
syndicated data on competitive media expenditures.

For *each* competitor (ideally for all of them, but at least for the major ones),
you must also find out the following:

- What is the company's financial position? This can be found by
looking at stock market information or Standard & Poors reports, where
available, or by obtaining a recent issue of the company's annual report.
- How does the competitor position its brand? To determine this, you
will have to use your own judgment. Examine the advertising for the
brand and see what is being emphasized. Is it similar to your own current
efforts, or not? If it is dissimilar, is that because there is an actual differ-

ence between the two brands, or do consumers just perceive a distinction between them? And who has the more favorable position?

• How does the competitor promote its brand? Which media are used? How much does the competitor spend to promote its brand? Where and when does it spend its money? The answers to these questions may come from several sources. Many large companies, and/or their agencies, subscribe to syndicated competitive spending data from either TNS-Sofres or Nielsen Monitor Plus. Both show, on a weekly, monthly, quarterly, and annual basis, how much money was spent by a brand in each major media category (see Exhibit 2.5). Smaller businesses may simply try to keep track of where their competitors' ads are appearing. This is not too difficult if you are dealing with a local product, but gets more complicated the wider the area that you or your competitors try to cover. You can also subscribe to a clipping service that will do the tracking for you (see Appendix A for more on this).

Share of Market.   Once you have looked at the trends for your brand and its competitors, you must then put that information together and see how your brand is faring in the marketplace. The percentage of total category sales that your brand enjoys is known as the *market share*. You should try to examine how this figure has changed over time. Have you been gaining or losing market share in the past few years? Again, be careful to avoid oversimplifying the picture. It could be that you have been losing market share, but because of the entry of several new brands into the category, so have your major competitors. We can see this in the media arena in television. Whereas 10 years ago the four broadcast networks commanded 90% of the prime time audience, today fewer than half of all viewers tune in to ABC, CBS, FOX, or NBC at that time, with the remainder watching cable networks.

Share of Requirements

One of the most useful pieces of information you can examine is the source of your brand's sales. This is known as the *share of requirements*. It is calculated by taking the percentage of total category volume accounted for by a particular brand's users. Quite simply, it tells you whether your brand is being bought primarily by your customers or by your various competitors' customers. And, conversely, how much of your competitors' sales are coming from your brand users. Looking at this figure, you will be able to determine what percentage of the volume that you sell is accounted for by your users, as opposed to people who usually buy another brand.

EXHIBIT 2.5   Example of competitive spending report

Selected Spending for Coca-Cola Company, January–June 2005

Parent Company	Brand	Total Dollars (000)	Network TV Dollars (000)	Spanish Language TV Dollars (000)	Cable TV Dollars (000)	Syndication TV Dollars (000)	Spot TV Dollars (000)	Magazine Dollars (000)	Business-to-Business Dollars (000)	National Newspaper Dollars (000)	Local Newspaper Dollars (000)	Hispanic Newspaper Dollars (000)	Network Radio Dollars (000)	Nat'l Spot Radio Dollars (000)	Local Radio Dollars (000)	Outdoor Dollars (000)
Coca-Cola	Coca-Cola Co. Corporate	$2,740.5	$638.8		$248.3		$0.8	$99.5	$902.0	$234.1	$548.5	$35.0			$33.6	
Coca-Cola	Coca-Cola Regular and Diet soft drink	$183.0								$183.0						
Coca-Cola	Coca-Cola Zero Soft Drink	$1,717.9	$1,579.0		$125.5		$10.5									$3.0
Coca-Cola	Dasani Bottled Water	$13,966.4	$10,097.7		$2,913.9		$5.2	$491.0					$359.0		$83.6	$16.1
Coca-Cola USA	Coca-Cola Bottlers	$372.7									$26.6	$15.4				$24.9
Coca-Cola USA	Coca-Cola C2 Soft Drink	$4,705.1	$3,090.6		$1,510.9	$43.0	$60.6									
Coca-Cola USA	Coca-Cola Classic Soft Drink	$83,442.0	$58,300.6	$9,402.3	$8,959.7	$4,180.9	$1,143.7	$399.6	$107.6				$512.6	$423.2	$305.9	$11.8

Source: Competitive Media Reporting, 2005

TABLE 2.1
Example of share of requirements

	Total Category Volume	Brand Share Volume	Brand Share of Requirements
National Pretzels	38%	25%	65%
Regional Pretzels	42	29	69
Pioneer Pretzels	27	15	55
Other Brands	9	5	65

Let's say you are a manufacturer of a local brand of pretzels (Pioneer Pretzels), competing with other regional brands as well as a major national brand. As you can see in Table 2.1, Pioneer Pretzels buyers account for 27% of all the pretzels sold in the last 30 days. Of all the pretzels they purchase, 15% of their usage is to your brand (Pioneer), and 12% is to other brands. This means that 55% (15% / 27%) of their total category volume is given to your brand, which gives Pioneer a 55% share of requirements. This is the lowest figure among all pretzel types, suggesting that Pioneer's users are not especially brand loyal, which could harm sales and future market share.

WHERE IS YOUR BRAND SOLD?

Once you have found out as much as possible about how your brand stacks up against the competition, you need to think about geographic and distribution considerations. Specifically, you must look at where your brand is selling well and where it is doing poorly both in terms of markets, regions, or states, and in terms of type of retail outlet. This holds true whether your brand is available on a national, regional, or local basis. Unless your product is sold in just one store or location, there are likely to be some differences in sales according to geography and distribution outlet. What you discover by looking at the sales for your brand in these ways may lead you to develop a media plan with regional or local differences.

Indeed, more marketers have adopted a regional approach to selling, realizing that people in Boise have different tastes, customs, and buying habits than people in Boston or Baton Rouge. So marketers are customizing their marketing and media plans (and, in some cases, their products) to meet the needs of specific areas of the country. Although some regional differences are obvious, such as higher snowblower sales in Maine than in Arizona, others might seem surprising (e.g., the fact that insecticides sell most heavily in the South). These types of differences occur not just at the product category level, but also for individual brands. Dannon yogurt sells far better on the East Coast than does Yoplait, which has traditionally been stronger in the West.

To understand geographic skews, the media specialist can turn to two pieces of information: development indices and market share.

Development Indices

You could, in theory, obtain sales data from every region or store in the country and look through them to find out your brand's sales picture. But a more efficient method for analyzing geographic strengths and weaknesses is to look at how the product category is doing across the United States and, then, how the brand is developing over time. Both of these are calculated by using *developmental indices*.

Category Development Index.   The category development index (CDI) looks at product category sales in each potential region or market. A norm, or average, is calculated at 100, and then each area is assigned a value relative to that, expressed as a percent. Numbers below 100 indicate the category has lower than average sales in a given region, whereas those above 100 suggest sales of the category are greater than the national average in a certain part of the country. If, on average, 30,000 tractors are sold per month per region across the United States, that might mean 25,000 units are sold in the East, 45,000 in the West, and 33,000 in the South. Eastern sales would index at 83 (25,000/30,000), meaning that sales in that area are 17% below the national norm, whereas sales in the West would have a CDI of 150 (45,000/30,000), indicating that that region's sales are 50% higher than average. Those in the South have a CDI of 110 (33,000/30,000), which shows that southern sales are 10% higher than the norm. Based on such information, a company might decide to concentrate its marketing and media efforts in those regions with higher CDIs, because that is where there is greater potential for all tractor sales.

Brand Development Index.   You should not rely solely on the CDI in making geographic media decisions, however. You also need to look at how your brand stacks up against other brands in the category. One tool for this job is the brand development index (BDI). The calculation is very similar to that of the CDI. You calculate a norm, or average, for all brands (or chief competitors) in the category, which is again set at 100, and then see how your own brand is doing in comparison. The John Deere tractor company might find its BDI for tractor sales is 10% above average in the eastern region and 5% below the norm in the West, suggesting that it is doing better than other brands in the category in the East, but slightly less well in comparison in the West.

When you look at the BDI, you need to keep the CDI in mind too. Once you have these two sets of data, you should compare your BDI to your CDI. In that way you will be able to find those markets where your brand is doing better than the category overall and, conversely, where your brand appears to be underperforming the category (see Exhibit 2.6). For John Deere, its eastern BDI is greater than the CDI, so the brand is doing better than the category in that region. In the West, however, its BDI is below the CDI, so there is room for improvement here.

Armed with this information, you may choose to adopt one of three possible marketing and media strategies. You can focus your attention on those areas of the country where your brand is doing better than the category, playing to your strengths. Or you might choose to give more attention (and money) to the weaker markets where the category is doing well but your brand isn't in an attempt to bolster your sales there. Alternatively, you might decide to play it safe and concentrate on markets where both category and brand are successful. The one strategy you should probably avoid is pouring money into areas where both brand and category are doing poorly, because that suggests there is something about all the brands that is not liked or does not meet the needs of those consumers. To try and rectify that situation single-handedly is probably going to be more trouble (and cost) than it is worth.

EXHIBIT 2.6 BDI versus CDI

		Category Index	
		High	Low
Brand Index	High	Both brand and category growing	Brand growing and category declining
	Low	Brand declining and category growing	Both brand and category growing

Market Share

When looking at the development indices you can also find out how your competition is doing in each territory and calculate their BDIs. It is common to see that where your brand is doing well, your competitors are having a harder time, and vice versa. The exception here would be for a new or relaunched category where all brands are selling well, such as flavored water.

One way of investigating sales further in geographic terms is to look at your share of the market by region or locality. Is your brand number one in sales in the Central region but in third place in the South? Are you neck-and-neck in New York, but a distant second in Florida? Faced with these different scenarios, you should explore some of the possible reasons behind the distinctions. And here you should go back to the other "Ps" of the marketing process. Perhaps you have *distribution* problems in Florida that are harming sales. Maybe your brand is being undercut in price in the South by a local manufacturer. Or it could be that your chief competitor is flooding the local airwaves with *promotional messages* in New York and drowning out yours. By putting together the information you gather from the development indices with your market share figures, you will start to create a picture of how your brand is doing across the country. That will help you decide what marketing and media tactics might be needed in each situation.

The media plan will not be the miracle solution to all of the problems you might encounter, and you should not expect it to turn a floundering brand into a superstar. But, as we shall see in subsequent chapters, the better your understanding of the marketing situation your brand is in, the more likely you are to come up with creative solutions to the problems. For example, if your problem is distribution, then you might want to include extra trade promotions or incentives in your plan to encourage retailers or distributors to push your brand further. Pricing discrepancies might be alleviated by offering a coupon or on-pack premium to offset the lower priced competitors. And if your consumers are being faced with a barrage of competitive messages in one medium, then it might be wise to consider placing your own advertising in completely different media, or perhaps move to non traditional media or special events to raise your own voice elsewhere.

Finally, if possible, you should try and look at your brand's geographic strengths and weaknesses over time to see where the trends are going. Have you always been weaker in the Southwest, or does this seem to have started only in the past year? Is the overall category development index flattening out across the country, or is it moving to different areas? This is especially likely to be true for new product categories when they are first introduced, as was the case when the low carbohydrate craze started. As always, looking at several years of data will help you to avoid acting on "blips" in the numbers that might have disappeared without cause within a few months.

CONSUMERS AND MEDIA

Although a successful marketing plan requires a thorough understanding of consumers' relationships with the brand, increasingly there is the realization that a similarly thorough knowledge is needed to learn how consumers interact with media. Subsequent chapters explore in greater detail the characteristics of each major media form, but here we introduce the notion of the value of media *context*, or environment.

As you start to learn more about the way consumers use and think about your brand, you can also begin to investigate how they use and think about media. Do your tractor owners, for example, rely on the early morning farming report on the radio? Are they going online to check on crop prices? With the Razor Sharp brand, are the men you want to reach with your message about its reusability interested in men's health and fitness magazines? If so, how do they read them and what do they think about them? And, in both cases, how do they respond to ads placed in those key media contexts, as compared to seeing the same message placed elsewhere?

The impact of context has long been explored by the academic community, primarily by looking at the effects of consumer involvement with the media in which ads appear. (Consult selection of articles.[3])

The advertising industry has more recently begun exploring media context. Agencies such as Starcom Mediavest Group, with its consumer context planning (CCP) function, or Media Kitchen with its communication planning approach are each recognizing that media should be thought of more from the consumers' viewpoint, and it is no longer enough to know basic media usage figures (how often a program is watched or a magazine read). Rather, consumers' relationships with the media can be critical to the way they respond to the brand message. The highly positive reaction to General Motors' Hummer H2 vehicle when it was introduced in 2003 was attributed

---

[3]"Editorial Environment and Advertising Effectiveness," Valentine Appel, *Journal of Advertising Research*, vol. 27, No. 4, August/September 1987, 11–16. "A Cross-Media Study of Audience Choice: The Influence of Media Attitudes on Individual Selection of 'Media Repertoires,'" Elizabeth Gigi Taylor and Wei-Na Lee, *Proceedings of the 2004 Conference of the American Academy of Advertising*, 39–48. "Magazine Reader Involvement Improves ROI," Britta C. Ware, *ESOMAR, Print Audience Measurement*, LA, June 2003. "The Medium Is Part of the Message," Maria Christina Moya Schilling, Karin Wood and Alan Branthwaite, *ESOMAR, Reinventing Advertising*, Rio, November 2000, 207–229

in part to the finding that the consumers being targeted had an extremely strong relationship with news-oriented media. The inclusion of more of that genre in the media plan, instead of the more traditional new vehicle launch of high-profile network television, helped H2 far surpass its first-year sales goals.

We shall return to the CCP concept throughout the discussion of media in this book.

A WORD ABOUT BUDGETS

One of the most important preplanning issues to look at is how much money you are likely to have to spend for media for the coming year. You may be given a specific amount upfront, or you may have a range within which to work. In many situations, the media specialist is likely to come up with two or three alternative media plans at different spending levels, showing what could be achieved with $500,000, versus $1 million, versus $2 million, for example. We will say more about this in chapter 7. If possible, try to be flexible on the budget at this point, keeping in mind that if you lock yourself into a set figure from the very beginning, then you may limit your creativity later on when you put the plan together.

TIMING AND OTHER ISSUES

The last major area to explore in the preplanning phase is that of timing. This may include the month of the year, the week of the month, the day of the week, or the hour of the day. Although some timing considerations can be rationalized and justified, others may be out of your control. Some companies skew their messages toward pay periods, such as the 15th and 30th of the month, knowing that people are more likely to spend money on paydays. Packaged-goods marketers may choose an end-of-week schedule to reflect the increase in grocery store shopping from Wednesday through Friday. Other considerations may be out of your control. The CEO of the company that makes your brand of sports drink may demand that you purchase television time during the Wimbledon tennis tournament. He not only likes tennis but wants to get tickets to the event. The marketing manager may refuse to have the brand advertised in any magazine that accepts cigarette advertisements. Perhaps your candy company has been a sponsor of a local parade for the past 50 years and you cannot break with that tradition.

There might also be key timing opportunities that you should consider. If you are going into a Summer or Winter Olympics year, then you might want to look for some way to tie your brand into that. Although this sounds out of the league of any but the largest national advertisers, there may be an Olympic swim team member in your own town whom your brand of swim goggles could support in some way. Or, if your city is celebrating its 200th anniversary and your pen factory has been around for almost as long, then you could get involved in the preparations for related events. If next year has been designated the Year of the Child, then you can look for opportunities to promote your diaper brand. Be alert and open to new ideas and opportunities such as these that might come along infrequently and sporadically but could greatly enhance your brand's profile and help sales locally, regionally, or even nationally.

SUMMARY

Before getting down to this year's plan it is important to know as much as possible about what has happened in the past. Find out as much as possible about how your company has operated in previous years, how your brand has performed, and what the competitors have done. Looking at trends in the product category is not only helpful, but might lead to new ways to define or position what you have to sell. Be aware of cultural, social, and economic forces that might impact your performance. As you examine your brand, consider who its real competitors are and learn about their past and present marketing plans. Determine your brand's share of market and share of requirements, too.

Preplanning should also include an analysis of geographic variations in sales through category and brand development indices. Think about how consumers purchase and use your brand, how aware they are of it and its advertising, and when and how much they actually buy.

As you learn more about consumers' relationship with your brand and its competitors, also consider how they respond to the media that are important to their lives. Examining the context, or environment, of your brand's messages can provide critical information early on in the planning process that will be helpful as you develop your plans. Finally, keep in mind any budgeting or timing constraints that will affect your media plan.

CHECKLIST—MEDIA IN THE MARKETING CONTEXT

1. Have you considered all elements of the marketing mix (price, place, product, and promotions)?
2. How much do consumers know about your brand?
3. Do you need to conduct research on your consumer through focus groups, surveys, or analysis of syndicated data?

4. When do consumers buy your product? Which time of year, month, day of week, or time of day?

5. How much do consumers buy? Is there a difference by product size or flavor?

6. Have you analyzed the history of your brand (how long it has been available, how successful it has been in the past, how it has been positioned in the past)? Include the company's history here too.

7. What are your brand's chief competitors doing?

8. What are the product category trends?

9. How is your brand faring compared to competitors in terms of market share and share of requirements?

10. How does each major competitor position its brand and promote it?

11. Have you calculated the category and brand development indices for your brand?

12. Are there regional differences for your brand's sales and market share?

13. Do your consumers have any special relationships with particular media that might affect their response to brand messages?

14. Have you considered any timing issues for the brand?

CHAPTER 3

Developing Optimal Media Objectives

Setting objectives is something we are all familiar with in our day-to-day lives. "I will get an 'A' on this test;" "I'll lose 10 pounds by Christmas;" "My goal is to become the CEO of the company by the time I reach 35." Whatever the objective may be, if you didn't have one, then it would be difficult to know what you've achieved!

In the media planning context, you need to establish firm objectives for your plan in order to demonstrate how it will help your brand achieve its marketing goals. Although you may feel that in order to execute a media plan you must keep returning to your starting point, moving one step back for every two you go forward, it cannot be overemphasized that *everything* you do on the media planning side must be coordinated with the overall marketing strategy. Therefore, in order to establish your media objectives (i.e., what you intend the media plan to achieve), you must first reaffirm and clarify the goals of your complete advertising program to ensure that your media objectives fit in with the goals set in your brand's marketing objectives.

HOW THE MARKETING OBJECTIVE LEADS TO THE MEDIA OBJECTIVE

Media specialists are likely to be presented with the marketing objective rather than having to develop it on their own. It is usually stated in some quantifiable form, such as "sell x thousand more widgets in 2006 than in 2005," or "increase awareness of Brand X to 75% within calendar year 2006." It may relate to any of the major marketing functions, such as increasing shelf space in the store, or increasing the number of distribution channels for your product. Frequently, it is expressed in terms of specific volume and share goals, such as "within calendar year 2006, bring Brand Z's total volume sold to 25% of the total category, raising its market share from 35% to 38%."

If the marketing objective is vague or ill-defined, simply "increasing awareness" or "improving distribution," then at the end of the year (or whatever time period has been set to achieve the goal) there is likely to be considerable debate over whether or not the plan was successful. It is also going to be more difficult for the media specialist to devise a plan that satisfies those objectives; even if awareness does improve, how much higher must it go in order for the media plan to be considered a success?

Along with understanding the marketing objective, the media specialist should also look at *how* that objective will be achieved, because that will affect what the media plan is supposed to do. Examples might be to increase product penetration among potential users by taking sales away from competitors or bringing new users into the marketplace. Alternatively, the strategy might be to encourage people to use your brand more frequently, perhaps offering new uses for it. In order to increase the sales of Ragu Spaghetti Sauce, the marketing objective might be to get current users to buy additional jars of the product for use in new and different ways besides just pouring it onto spaghetti. For the media plan, this could lead to an objective of increasing the frequency with which target users are exposed to the message to remind them of the various ways they can use the product.

For a hospital with the marketing objective of introducing a new children's critical care unit and encouraging more people in the community to choose that facility for their pediatric medical needs, the media objective could be to reach 75% of people who live within a 10-mile perimeter to inform them of what is now available. Clearly, the marketing objective has a major impact on how the media plan develops, affecting the target audience, communications used, and media selected.

MEDIA AND THE ADVERTISING OBJECTIVE

As noted earlier, the marketing objective may relate to any of the four major areas of the marketing mix (product, promotion, distribution, or price). Therefore, before establishing specific media objectives, it is also essential to focus on how the media affect your advertising goals. Although your ultimate *marketing* goal for most goods is to sell more product (or services or image), unless your audience finds out about the product through the media that you use, that goal is unlikely to be reached. You need to be aware, at the same time, of the other marketing mix elements. If the product is no good, then your media advertising will have little impact. Similarly, if you advertise your product heavily but it isn't available in most stores, then sales will not improve.

Frequently, the objective of your advertising is tied in to the stage at which the target audience is in the decision-making process. As noted earlier, this process breaks down into three very broad areas: Think, Feel, and Do (or, in research-speak, the *cognitive, affective,* and *conative* stages). Once you have decided that you need a new TV set, you will *think* about what brands are available. Then you will consider how you *feel* about each one of them. And, finally, you will select a particular brand and take action (*do*) and buy it.

This process can be better understood by revisiting the eight main stages of the consumer decision-making process introduced in chapter 2:

1. Need.
2. Awareness.
3. Preference.
4. Search.
5. Selection.
6. Purchase.
7. Use.
8. Satisfaction.

Need

Before you can hope to sell any more widgets, people need a reason to buy them. Contrary to what many advertising critics maintain, advertising cannot persuade people to buy something they do not want. Indeed, it is often easier to think of this first stage in the decision process as reflecting people's *wants,* because in today's industrial society most people are able to satisfy their basic needs (e.g., food and shelter).

Even when people buy products that seem pointless or silly, such as chia pets or hula hoops, they may feel they have a *need* to indulge in it just for fun. And although you might argue that no one really has a *need* for a $150,000 BMW, the individuals who choose to purchase one clearly feel that they deserve this luxury automobile. Defining what the need might be for the product helps the marketer to understand the motivations behind why people might buy it, which in turn may provide some clues as to ways of reaching those people through the media. Although everyone buys shampoo, if you can segment the target into different groups according to their motivation for use, then you could reach each one through a variety of media forms. People who are most concerned with how their hair looks may be reached in fashion and beauty magazines. Those who want a shampoo with built-in conditioner to help in their busy lives may respond to ads in women's maga-

zines that offer advice on juggling multiple roles. For those who need shampoo designed specifically for dry (or oily or easily tangled) hair, then print
ads explaining the specific benefits might be more appropriate. And all of
that is just within magazines. Research conducted directly with target consumers may reveal that different segments have different media habits altogether, leading you, as planner, to determine what those media options
should be. This is covered in greater details in subsequent chapters, but you
should understand how different needs can often lead to different media
choices.

Awareness

Once consumers have determined that they need a particular product, it is
the job of marketing to make them aware of the available choices. For the
media specialist, this means reaching that consumer in the right place and
often enough so that your brand's message is the most relevant and convincing. And it is not enough to simply make people aware of your *brand;*
the real goal here is to make them aware of your brand's *message.* You might
well be able to reach 95% of all cat owners to make them aware of the new cat
food that you sell, but unless they also learn that your product provides
100% of a cat's daily nutritional requirement, which is more than any other
competitor, then your advertising is unlikely to increase sales. Of course,
keep in mind that although you are promoting *your* message, every other
cat food company is also trying to boost awareness of its own brand.

Preference

Based on the various choices consumers see and hear, they will then develop specific brand preferences. Ideally, marketers would like a consumer
to develop *brand loyalty* to their brand so that every time Julie Smith needs to
buy more running shoes, for example, she always chooses Saucony. A media
plan to enhance preference might include opportunities for the target audience to try your brand at home, perhaps by offering a free sample in magazines or via the Internet.

Search

Once the target audience decides it might prefer your brand over others,
the audience's next task is to find out where to purchase the item. Here, media advertising can be a big help by notifying people of the places that sell
your product. You have probably seen or heard this yourself in local or regional TV and radio ads that list which stores in your area stock the item.
Billboards can be used as well to display the retailer's or dealer's name. A

web ad can link directly to a local seller of your product. If your audience cannot find the product when it wants to buy it, then not even the best advertising placed in the most appropriate media will help increase sales.

Selection

Brand selection may seem like an easy stage for the consumer. If a woman has decided already that she prefers Cover Girl nail polish over others, and has learned that it is sold in Wal-Mart stores, then isn't it obvious that she will buy it? Not necessarily. Today's consumer is faced with so many different brands that, once in the store and standing in front of the shelf, she may decide to go with the competitor's offering, because it is on sale, it is packaged more attractively, or it comes in larger bottles. So the selection process is a crucial stage for the marketer and the media specialist to consider. From a media perspective, the nail polish user may be encouraged by in-store vehicles such as in-pack premiums or point-of-purchase radio. Personal contacts can also be very important at this stage. Someone who has come into the store in order to buy a midrange computer may be encouraged to select your more expensive model by being offered one year of free parts and service by the dealer.

Purchase and Use

Clearly, the ultimate goal of marketing and media plans is to persuade consumers to purchase the product. But if they buy it and never use it, then there is no reason for them to ever buy another one. No marketer can remain successful by continually targeting new product users. Often, one marketing and media objective is that of encouraging consumers to *use* the brand. In media planning terms, this might involve increasing the message frequency so that users are reminded of the different ways in which the brand can be used. A good example of this, in past years, has been Campbell's soup, which often places recipes in its print ads to encourage people to use more of the product, and hence purchase it more frequently.

Satisfaction

The final stage in the consumer decision process is really a feedback loop into the earlier ones. If people come to your restaurant but are dissatisfied with the quality of the food or friendliness of the staff, then their dissatisfaction will likely mean they won't return to your venue again. What is worse, they may tell their friends about their bad experience and decrease your potential sales even further. So customer satisfaction is extremely important for future success. *Satisfaction* is generally not listed as the primary marketing or media objective of a plan, but it should nonetheless be kept in mind when deciding where and when to place an advertising message. It is perhaps harder to achieve through the media, because it is ultimately up to the users to decide whether or not they are satisfied. But many advertisers promise "satisfaction guaranteed or your money back" as a way to reassure consumers that they will, indeed, be content if they buy your brand.

ADVERTISING OBJECTIVES AND THE CONSUMER DECISION PROCESS

To see how advertising objectives might fit in with each stage of the consumer decision process, let's take an example. If your client is the city's professional soccer team trying to increase the number of people who attend home games, then you may not have to create a "need" for your offering, because anyone who likes sports feels like the need to attend live games. It is very likely, however, that you would want to increase awareness of your team. So your advertising objective might be to boost awareness of the Soccer Stars from a baseline measure of 40% to 70% among young people under 25 within a 50-mile radius of the city.

It could be that many people have heard about your team, but they are still choosing to attend baseball games instead. Here, your advertising objective would be to improve *preference,* so that instead of 2 out of 10 under 25s choosing to go to a soccer game over baseball, 3 out of 10 do so. Setting advertising objectives for the subsequent stages in the decision process is somewhat less common because it is believed that advertising has a less direct role to play here. But you still want to encourage your target to *use* your team by attending games. Your advertising objective would be to boost visits to your games from an average of one time per year to four, perhaps by promotional tickets or special events at the stadium.

MEDIA AND THE CONSUMER DECISION PROCESS

The advertising media will also affect each of these stages in the consumer decision process. To continue with the Soccer Stars example, you might boost *awareness* of the team through widespread local TV and radio ads or outdoor billboards in the communities where you believe there are high concentrations of young adults. Consumer *preference* could be encouraged by sending direct mail to potential visitors offering them two tickets for the price of one. They could be helped in the *search* process by putting ads that provide maps to your stadium in local newspapers. *Selection* might be helped by bringing some of the bigger soccer stars in from out of town and offering the opportunity for fans to meet them. These special events could then be promoted in local media and perhaps receive additional publicity through press releases. Finally, to get current team supporters to *use* the team and attend more games, you might create a monthly newsletter that tells them about the exciting events coming up at future games.

Let's take another example. Say you are in the market for a new automobile. That puts you in the initial stages of *needing* a new car. You see some TV ads for various makes and models, increasing your awareness of what is available. Three of the cars that interest you are the Honda Accord, the Ford 500, and the Chevy Malibu Maxx. You read several automotive magazines, check out their resale value on Edmunds.com, and pick up the *Consumer Reports* issue on new cars. You decide that these models fit your needs. Now you have developed a *preference* for these particular models out of the hundreds that are available. Your next step would be to visit some car dealerships to *search* out the cars themselves. Here, your interaction with the salespeople is likely to play a major role in influencing your decision. You will also probably talk to friends and colleagues and return to the Internet to look in greater detail at each car's specifications. Faced with all of the information you have gathered, you *select* the Maxx. You negotiate a deal and drive the car home; now you can *use* it, and based on your experiences, you will develop a degree of *satisfaction* with your new purchase. If you are happy with this car, then you may well buy another Chevrolet the next time you are in the car market.

The media's role is important at several points in the process. Television advertising is frequently used to create or enhance *awareness,* informing people of the qualities of the brand and what it has to offer. And increasingly, in-program placement of products within TV shows are being used for these same reasons. Both TV and magazines can help develop consumer *preference*. Here, you might see ads that compare the Chevy Malibu to other cars in the same class, or that cite the awards and rankings the car has received in automotive competitions. And as already noted, personal contacts and the Internet may be critical too. Retail or local ads on spot radio, television, and outdoor billboards help reach consumers who are *searching* for your brand; sometimes you will see a brief message from the local dealership tagged on to the end of a commercial.

To encourage people to *select* your offering, the media may offer special discounts or added features, such as a 60,000 mile warranty or $1,000 cash back. Getting people to *use* the product is also important. Although this is not an issue in the case of an automobile, it can be for other consumer products. Nestle, for instance, uses print ads that feature recipes for foods made with its Toll House chocolate chips in order to encourage people to take the product off the shelf.

As with the marketing objective, the more measurable the advertising objective, the easier it will be to determine whether it has been achieved. This can be done either through specific testing after the ads have run for a while, or by setting up some kind of market test and determining the effect of advertising on sales.

CONSUMERS, BRANDS, AND MEDIA

Both advertising and media objectives require a clear understanding of how consumers connect with brands and with media. This relationship can be thought of as a Venn diagram, or a series of connecting circles. That is, consumers relate to certain brands, and are more likely to be receptive to those brands' advertisements when they appear in the media forms that the consumer likes and/or responds to. Exhibit 3.1 displays this relationship.

What some advertisers and agencies have realized in recent years is that the advertising industry has typically focused on just two of the three circles at any one time. That is, the media department has zoomed in on the relationship of consumers to media, whereas the agency account planning and client brand management departments have concentrated efforts on exploring consumers' relationships with brands. To truly fulfill advertising and media objectives, however, those three elements must all be examined together.

As noted in chapter 2, this practice (known variously as consumer context planning, the consumer-centric approach, or communications planning) involves in-depth research (qualitative and/or quantitative) to understand in greater depth who the target audience is, and how they relate to both the brands they use and the media they consume. The approach has been embraced by large marketers such as General Motors and Procter & Gamble, who spend significant funds on learning about that relationship of

EXHIBIT 3.1   Relationship of brands, media, and comsumers

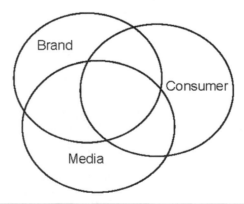

brand–media–consumer for their products, whether a Cadillac luxury vehicle or Kotex pantyliners. The concept is examined more closely as we go through the rest of the media planning process.

ESTABLISHING MEDIA OBJECTIVES

Armed with clear and concise marketing and advertising objectives that are in sync with how your brand's consumers think about and respond to the brand and to media, you are now ready for the most important part of the media planning process—setting media objectives. As with the other goals, once you have a clearly defined course set for you, it becomes much easier to figure out how to get there. There are three main elements involved in the media objectives: defining the target audience, setting broad communication objectives, and considering creative requirements.

Defining the Target Audience

Although you haven't yet started to put a plan together, you are probably beginning to realize that much of the most important work needs to be done beforehand to establish the media objectives. Defining the target audience is one key step you must take in the objective-setting process, because only by knowing who you wish to reach through the media will you be able to put together a schedule that will convey your brand's message to the right people.

Ideally, the target audience for your media plan should be identical to the audience for the overall marketing plan. Most of a brand's sales are typically generated by its current users, so the target audience definition is likely to include some product usage qualification. A marketing plan intended to increase sales of Pantene shampoo–conditioner combinations might have as its target audience "women 25 to 54 who currently use shampoo-conditioners, with an annual household income of more than $50,000." Life stage can be a crucial factor too. A plan geared toward increasing awareness of your new Sony digital camcorder might have as its target "adults 25 to 49 who have had a child in the past year."

Often, however, you will find that the media target may be both more and less precise than the marketing target. This is largely because the media themselves have traditionally been bought and sold on the basis of fairly basic demographics, such as age, sex, income, education, or race. For example, whereas your brand of Carr's crackers may be aiming to sell 20,000 more packets this year by expanding its user base and capturing more sales from "young adult gourmet lovers who enjoy entertaining and eating out," when it comes to creating your media objectives, your target may be "adults 18 to 34 with college education and an annual household income of more than $30,000." This is a more precise definition in that it specifies a particular age category as well as particular income and education levels, but it does not take into account (at least definitionally) the lifestyle variables (like eating out, entertaining, and fine foods).

It is also worth pointing out that the media target should be identical to the creative target. Although this may seem blatantly obvious, occasionally the research and account teams will develop a complex and precise target audience, but the creative team will march forward with its own ideas of who the message should speak to. That leaves the media department in confusion. So just as the media specialists should have seen and understood the marketing objectives, they should also be familiar with the Creative Brief, a document that lays out for the copywriter and art director the fundamental information about who or what the brand is, what the communication goals are for the campaign, and, importantly, who the message is directed at. Ideally, all of the target definitions will match!

As far as media definitions of targets are concerned, the syndicated data sources of audience information are usually the first port of call. Depending on the target, these resources may provide armloads of information; or they may offer up next to nothing. In particular, if you are dealing with a nonconsumer target, such as retailers or dealers, you may find yourself without much syndicated information at all, relying more on your experience and judgment. You can assume, for example, that if you are trying to promote your refrigeration equipment to restaurants, then one place to put your message would be *Restaurant News*.

One important consideration for defining your media target is whether it should be broad or narrow. Because everyone in the country uses laundry detergent, does that mean your media plan should be aimed at "all adults in the United States who use laundry detergent"? Increasingly, the answer will be "no." Today's brands are becoming more segmented. So there is not just one box of Tide on the store shelf, but 11 varieties, including powder or liquid Tide, Tide with Bleach, or Tide Cold Water Wash. There are 20 different sizes of Tide Liquid alone, aiming to suit the needs of diverse groups, from singles living alone to large families. Each of these groups is likely to have different media habits and preferences, and trying to create a media plan that would reach everyone would ignore the needs of different population groups both in terms of product benefits and media usage. There might be one plan aimed at mothers with young children, another for those with large families, another with an environmental slant, and a fourth promoting the smaller size for urban apartment dwellers. Each plan has a different target audience.

There is also the opposite danger, however. That is, you might define your target audience so narrowly that it would be almost impossible to reach them. You might, after checking previous research into who buys your large screen TVs, find that these individuals are most likely to be college-educated graduates of private colleges, professionals working in high-tech industries, living in the western region in A counties or suburbs in homes worth $150,000 or more, with 3+ children, and with at least 3 TV sets in their homes (see Exhibit 3.2). But there may be only a few hundred of them!

There are two major problems here. First, most traditional media will not only present your message to *your* target, but also to many others for whom the product is probably irrelevant. This is a problem that can only be alleviated by careful consideration of exactly who your target should be and which media will best reach that audience. Again, thinking of all three parts of the connecting circles will help you here, because with a thorough understanding of how your target relates not just to your brand but to the media they consume, your media plan is not only more likely to reach that target but it will do so more effectively.

Exhibit 3.2 Profile of big screen TV owner

People who own a big screen TV are:

more likely to	less likely to
be ...	**be ...**
Age 25-54	Age 65+
College educated	High school graduates
Male	Female
Suburban	Rural
Living in Pacific region	Living in Northeast region
read magazines on	**read magazines on**
Cars	Hunting & fishing
Travel	History & science
listen to ...	**listen to ...**
Adult Contemporary	Classical
News radio	Easy listening
watch ...	**watch ...**
College sports	Movies on TV
Sitcoms	Sunday morning talk shows
Late night talk shows	
watch pay/digital cable	watch broadcast TV
subscribe to digital cable/satellite TV	not subscribe to additional TV services

A second consideration in establishing media objectives is the cost effectiveness of the plan. It may well be the chief concern of you or of the top executives of your company. You could come up with an extremely elaborate and highly targeted media plan, with a clearly defined target audience and appropriate communication objectives, but if it is going to cost twice as much as is in the marketing budget, then you are unlikely to be able to execute it. When defining the target audience, you must be sure that the audience will be reachable at an affordable cost. The maker of Oral B toothbrushes cannot hope to reach everyone who brushes their teeth on a budget of $10 million.

Having defined your target audience, your next step should be to find out as much as possible about the individuals who make up that audience through primary and/or secondary research. Ideally, you should not only know their basic demographic characteristics (age, sex, education level, income, profession, etc.), but also learn more about the kinds of products they use and the media they tend to hear or see. Depending on the target, you can often obtain this information from syndicated data services. Or you may have to rely on your own judgment and experience. So if your target for an iPod is young adults between age 18 and 34 who listen to music, then you should also know that they are more likely to have a mobile phone and a DVD player, both of which may be effective advertising media forms.

Communication Objectives

When it comes to writing down what you expect the advertising message to do for your brand, you will start to find that all of a sudden you are dealing with the art, rather than the science, of media planning. These objectives are measurable to some degree through communications tests with the target audience that find out what information the audience is taking away from the message. In addition, media calculations can be made to estimate what the plan should achieve. But many of the criteria you need to use to establish what the goals should be are far more evaluative and rely on your judgment and subjective response to everything that you know about the brand, its advertising, and the marketplace. These objectives must also be in line with the overall marketing strategy for the brand. If you are trying to increase your market share of the athletic shoe category by 2 percentage points by increasing distribution into mass merchandise outlets, then your communication objective might involve increasing awareness of your brand among your target audience by 15% within the first 3 months of the campaign.

Communication objectives will vary, depending on the kind of product you are promoting. For launching a new brand of cat litter, you probably want your advertising to generate awareness of the product. If you are advertising Maytag dishwashers, in contrast—which have been around for-ever—your message will more likely serve as a reminder to consumers of the product's reliability. These differing objectives will also affect your reach and frequency goals. For a new product, you would want to establish some initial awareness levels and then sustain them (e.g., generate awareness of the product among 75% of the target group within the first 3 months of the campaign).

Don't forget to consider your competition too. You might set as your ob-jective to achieve, within the first 6 months of your new campaign, aware-ness levels for your Cannondale mountain bike that are equal to or greater than those of your closest competitor. Geography is another factor. If your bike is the number one brand in the category with the highest awareness lev-els in the northeast and pacific, but falls to number two or three in the south, then you might set different objectives in different parts of the country, broadening your reach in areas where awareness levels are currently lower.

There are three main factors to consider when developing communica-tion objectives: campaign timing, category and brand dynamics, and media reach and frequency.

Campaign Timing. This is the point where you should consider the stage of your campaign: Are you launching a new product, changing the strategy for selling it, or is this the third or fourth year of an ongoing cam-paign? Also, think about the specific timing of the campaign. Are you trying to communicate a seasonal message to warn young adults about drinking and driving during the holidays? Or maybe it's April and people are start-ing to think about summer vacation, so it's the perfect time to begin promoting your park district's swimming pool. Thinking of your communi-cations objectives within a specific timeframe will help to ensure that your media plan stays focused on that period.

Category and Brand Dynamics. If you study the trends for your brand in particular as well as trends within the category overall, then your commu-nication objectives will be firmly fixed in reality. That is, if research shows that users of lawn-care products are extremely brand loyal, then it makes lit-tle sense to say the objective for Scott's weed-killer is to gain 15 mar-ket-share points from your competitors in the next 12 months. Related to loyalty, you should also think about what degree of consumer involvement with the category can be reasonably expected. It's hard to get people ex-cited about staplers or canned tomatoes, no matter how wonderful your cre-ative message or media plan. Try to be objective about your brand's positioning too. Is your advertising message really very different from your competitors', or is it in fact just another version of the same idea? If you look at the advertising for most products, you'll see that the latter is far more common than the former. Almost all banks tout their low financing rates, nearly all beers talk about great taste, and most garbage bags emphasize their strength. None of this should be too surprising; you wouldn't want to buy a beer that didn't taste good or a garbage bag that wasn't strong.

Reach and Frequency.   Having stated earlier that communication objectives tend to be more subjective than objective, more art than science, there is still a role for some numbers here. But they should only be included if you will have some way of measuring them. The two key concepts to consider here are *reach* and *frequency*. These are the two most commonly used media terms in the whole planning process. The *reach* of the plan refers to the number (or percentage) of the target audience that will be reached by the brand's advertising in the media. As is explained in chapter 5, that number is determined by calculating what percentage of the target audience will be exposed to the media in which your ad appears. Along with knowing how many people will have the opportunity to see or hear your ad, you also need to state how many times they need to do so in order for the message to have some effect. This is the concept of *effective frequency.* You should identify some reach and frequency goals as a way of measuring whether or not your communication objectives were achieved. If the communication goal is to "increase awareness of the brand by 10% among the key consumer target," then that can be measured by establishing what percentage of the target was actually reached with the message and how many times they heard it, and whether brand awareness levels did in fact go up. More is said on this topic in chapter 5.

Creative Requirements

The last area that should be considered in preplanning discussions is any special creative requirement that will affect the media selected. As noted previously, this should be made evident in the Creative Brief, and provides another reason why it is critical for media specialists to be exposed to that document. If, for example, you are introducing a new hybrid car and want to talk about its advanced engineering and environmental benefits through long copy and details, then you will have to think in terms of the media that can allow you to do that. Or, if your task is to promote the Florida Keys as a vacation destination for families, then the creative requires media that convey the desired image by depicting many different sights or sounds from that area, such as print or the Internet, TV or radio. The message will, in part, determine where you choose to place it. Yet another example might be introducing a new Pillsbury cake mix. Your ads will showcase the delicious results of using the product, so the visual element is going to be particularly important. Immediately, this leads you in a certain direction when starting to consider your media plan strategies and tactics.

SUMMARY

In order for a media plan to be successful, it must be tied directly to the broad marketing objectives for the brand, usually defined in terms of sales and market share. The goals for media should also be derived from the advertising objectives, which show where the advertising fits in to the consumer's decision process, such as increasing awareness or improving customer satisfaction, or generating additional use of the product. Both marketing and advertising objectives are tied to the media objectives by considering the relationship that exists between consumers, brands, and media. The media objectives state to whom the message is to be delivered (the target audience), when it is to be distributed (timing specifics), and how many times a given proportion of the target will, ideally, be exposed (media reach and frequency). Special creative requirements for the brand's communications should also be taken into account, in part by ensuring that media specialists are able to review the Creative Brief.

CHECKLIST—DEVELOPING OPTIMAL MEDIA OBJECTIVES

1. Do you know your brand's marketing objectives?
2. Are they stated clearly and explicitly, in an actionable way?
3. What is the advertising objective for the brand?
4. Have you considered where the advertising might fit in with the eight stages of the consumer decision process—need, awareness, preference, search, selection, purchase, use, and satisfaction?
5. What have you learned about how consumers relate to your brand and the media they consume?
6. In which stage of the consumer decision process does your advertising objective fit?
7. Have you clearly defined your target audience, or audiences?
8. Are your target definitions in line with those developed by the marketing team and the creative team?
9. What are your communication objectives, in terms of a specific timeframe, given the competitive situation?
10. What are your media reach and frequency goals?
11. Are there any specific creative requirements for the brand's message?
12. Have you seen the Creative Brief?

CHAPTER 4

Exploring the Media

We are all familiar with television, radio, the Internet, newspapers, or magazines from the consumer's standpoint. That is, we don't think twice about picking up the newspaper every morning, listening to the radio on the way to work, going online to look up a specific Web site, watching TV when we get home at night, and leafing through a magazine in bed before going to sleep. For advertisers, each of those points of contact represents an opportunity to communicate with potential targets for their product or service. So, for example, the local car dealer will place his ad for a GMC Envoy in the daily newspaper in hope that you will see it in the morning and stop in at the dealership on the way home from work or over the weekend. The First National Bank might put an ad on the radio in the morning hours to reach commuters on their way to work to alert them to the bank's favorable interest rates on savings accounts. When you sit back and relax in the evening to watch television, a wide range of advertisers will remind you of their brand of beer, cookies, pet food, or coffee, either in traditional commercials or by placing their products within the programs themselves, hoping that on your next visit to the grocery store you will select their brand. And, finally, right before you fall asleep, advertisers in magazines will try to persuade you that their credit card company will be there when you need it.

MEDIA AS BRAND CONTACTS

The task of today's media planners has become much broader than in times past. Instead of just considering the traditional media (i.e., TV, radio, magazines, newspapers, outdoor), the planner now must evaluate all forms of "brand contact," wherever or however they occur. Should Kraft Macaroni and Cheese sponsor the local Little League teams? Can Columbia Sportswear be the official sponsor of an Olympic ski team? Would it make sense to put Powerbar ads along running trails? Should the detectives in *Law & Order* be shown drinking Coca-Cola? Or could Campbell Soup ads pop up on the Web site weather.com whenever the temperature falls below freezing in the location being viewed? The key with all of these communications is that they must be integrated with the traditional plan. That is, Powerbar's trails message should look and feel like its magazine ads, and should appear in the plan as another regular line item, scheduled in conjunction with all other media. And, as with all media planning elements, the selections must tie fully into the brand's marketing and media objectives.

MEDIA CATEGORIES

With the brands perspective in media, and with set media objectives in place, once you have clearly defined media objectives, the next step will be to decide which media types, and vehicles within those types, will best help you achieve your goals. Before exploring that further, we need to think about what the different media can offer you as an advertiser conveying an advertising message. Here, we will consider the six major media categories: television, radio, Internet, magazines, newspapers, and out-of-home. A seventh, broader category of "alternative" forms of media will round out the chapter.

As noted in chapter 1 there are various ways of categorizing the media. We can contrast the *print* media of magazines, newspapers, and outdoor billboards with *electronic* media (i.e., radio, Internet, and TV). We can also make an important distinction between media that are predominantly *local* (e.g., newspapers, outdoor billboards, and radio) and those where most ads are placed on a *national* basis (e.g., TV, Internet, and magazines). And, increasingly, we can classify media based on the level of consumer *control* involved in their use, from magazines, TV via DVRs, and the Internet, which require active involvement, to radio and traditional TV, which are more passively consumed. Here, we will look at the major characteristics of each media form.

A TELEVISION IN EVERY HOME

Almost every household in America has a television set, and three-quarters (75%) have two or more. The average household owns 2.4 TV sets. More than 9 in 10 homes (94%) operate their TV sets via remote control. Television is the largest mass medium available for advertisers. In 2004, about $68 billion was spent promoting goods and services this way. People in the United States have their TV sets on, on average, 7½ hours each day, which is one of the highest viewing figures of anywhere in the world. The average household can receive 93 channels, thanks to cable television. That figure continues to rise, increasing by 7 channels in just one year from 2003 to 2004.

Broadcast television programming is traditionally divided up in two ways: by *daypart* and by *format*. The daypart refers to the time of day the program airs. There are nine standard dayparts, which are shown in Exhibit 4.1. Program formats are also standardized into 14 main types, which are given in Exhibit 4.2. It is worth emphasizing that these breakdowns are really only the concern of the programmers and advertisers; you don't choose to watch "situation comedies" or "reality-based programs," but rather decide to watch *The Apprentice* on NBC on a specific night.

EXHIBIT 4.1 Dayparts		
Early Morning	M-F	7:00-9:00 a.m.
Daytime	M-F	9:00 a.m.-4:30 p.m.
Early Fringe	M-F	4:30-7:30 p.m.
Prime Access	M-F	7:30-8:00 p.m.
Primetime	M-S	8:00-11:00 p.m.
	Sun	7:00-11:00 p.m.
Late News	M-Sun	11:00-11:30 p.m.
Late Night	M-Sun	11:30 p.m.-1:00 a.m.
Saturday Morning	Sat	8:00 a.m.-1:00 p.m.
Weekend Afternoons	Sat-Sun	1:00-7:00 p.m.

Source: Nielsen Media Research, 2002.

EXHIBIT 4.2 Television program formats
Animation/children
Daytime serials
Drama/adventure
Game shows
Late-night talk
Movies
News
Newsmagazines
Reality-based
Sitcoms
Specials
Sports

Source: Nielsen Media Research, 2002.

The popularity of different program genres changes over time. Typically, the two most popular types are dramas and situation comedies. In the mid-1990s, newsmagazines (e.g., ABC's *20/20* and NBC's *Dateline*) became extremely popular, in part because the networks realized they were relatively inexpensive to make. The average prime-time drama can cost more than a million dollars per episode, as compared to a few hundred thousand for a newsmagazine.

More recently, reality programs such as *The Apprentice* and *American Idol* took hold, leading to many copycat programs and an overabundance of that program type. Although those programs continue to do well, viewers were seemingly bored with too much of just one format, and so the networks developed more dramas and sitcoms, such as *Desperate Housewives* and *Grey's Anatomy*. The challenge for media planners and, particularly, media buyers is to predict which shows will be popular several months, or even one year from now, buying them at a less expensive cost and enjoying higher-than-predicted ratings. We explore this further in chapter 8.

How people watch TV is changing, however, as more viewers acquire digital video recorders (DVRs) that allow them, in effect, to become their own program scheduler. By making it easy to record favorite shows, and fast-forward or pause both live and recorded programming, DVR providers (e.g., Tivo and the cable companies) have helped turn television from a passive medium where viewers watch what is shown when it appears, to a much more active experience where people can watch whatever they want whenever they wish to do so. The consequences of this for advertising is explored further in this chapter.

What people watch is also impacted by who owns the various TV networks. For example, Disney's ownership of ABC, Lifetime, and ESPN networks is not only evident in that ESPN announcers appear on ABC sports programming, but leads to *Wonderful World of Disney* on ABC. Likewise, CBS's *Survivor* stars appear the next morning on its *Morning Show*. Exhibit 4.3 shows the ownership of the major networks. Note that the ownership situation is never static. As this edition was going to press, Viacom spun off CBS television as a separate company, and CBS and Time Warner agreed to merge UPN and WB networks into a new network called CW, to launch in September 2006.

There are four main types of television to consider: network, syndication, spot (local), and cable. Beginning in the mid-1990s, the ownership of these various entities became more consolidated so that today just a handful of large media companies has majority control of all four types of TV, squeezing out the independents or mom-and-pop operations that flourished in the first 50 years of television. Viewers are not really aware of who owns what and they do not differentiate, for the most part, between network, cable, or syndication. They choose to watch a certain program,

EXHIBIT 4.3 Media company ownership

Rank	Company Name	TV	Print	Cable/Satellite	Internet	Radio	Outdoor	Cinema	Other
1	Time Warner	Turner Broadcast Systems, Home Box Office, WB	Time Inc magazines, Southern Progress Corp., Time4Media	Time Warner Cable	America Online			Warner Brothers, New Line Cinema	
2	Comcast Corp.	Golf Channel, Outdoor Life, E! Networks		Comcast Cable					
3	Viacom	MTV Networks, BET Holdings, Showtime Networks, CBS TV, UPN				Westwood One, Infinity Broadcasting	Viacom Outdoor	Paramount Pictures	Paramount Parks, King World Syndication, Simon & Schuster Publishing
4	Walt Disney Co.	ABC TV, Disney/ABC Cable, ESPN, A&E, Lifetime	Buena Vista Magazines, US Weekly			ABC Radio		Walt Disney Studios, Touchstone, Buena Vista Home Entertainment	Disney Stores, Disney Theme Parks, Baby Einstein, Disney Cruise Lines
5	NBC Universal	NBC TV, Telemundo, USA Network, CNBC, Sci Fi, Bravo, Trio, MSNBC, Pax TV						Universal Studios	Universal Studio Theme Parks

6	Cox Enterprises	Discovery Communications	Cox Newspapers	Cox Television	Cox Radio		
7	News Corp.	Fox Broadcasting, Fox Cable, National Geographic, TV Guide Channel, DirecTV					20th Century Fox, Fox Searchlight
8	Gannett Co.	Gannett Broadcasting	Gannett Newspapers, USA Weekend				
9	Clear Channel Communications	Clear Channel Television			Clear Channel Radio	Clear Channel Outdoor	Harper Collins Publishers
10	Advance Publications	Bright House Networks	Advance Newspapers, Parade, Conde Nast, Golf Digest, Fairchild Publications, American City Business Journals				

Source: Advertising Age, 8/14/04

regardless of how or where it airs, or who created it or owns it. So the distinctions we draw here are purely for media purposes.

Network Television

Network television consists of four major broadcast networks: ABC, CBS, NBC, and FOX. There are also two smaller networks: UPN (now owned by CBS) and WB. A "network" is actually made up of hundreds of local stations that become "affiliates" of the national organization. There are a total of 1,276 network affiliate stations, about half of all TV stations on air (2,482). Each station receives a set amount of money every year from the network in return for which they agree to air national programs for a given number of hours every week. But, as the networks have looked for ways to cut their costs in recent years, they have attempted to cut or eliminate these payments. Network programs air at the same time in every market within a given time zone. So CBS's "60 Minutes" appears at 7 p.m. on Sunday night in the Eastern zone, 6 p.m. in Central markets, and 5 p.m. in the Mountain zone. Programs in the Pacific time zone are shown at the same time locally as in the East (i.e., *60 Minutes* airs at 7 p.m. Pacific time).

Network shows come with several minutes of commercial time both within and between programs that are sold by the network. The local station is then able to sell an additional 1 to 3 minutes of commercial time in the hour to local or regional advertisers, depending on the daypart. Historically, local commercials always had to appear in the commercials that aired between programs, but that rule has been relaxed, allowing local or regional advertising within the program too. The research findings on the relative effectiveness of ads appearing between or within programs has been mixed. The local station also decides what to air when it is not showing network programs. This might include locally produced shows, such as local news or current affairs programs, or programs purchased from independent producers, known as syndicated programming (see next section).

Stations not affiliated with a network are known as *independents*. Today, there are only 88 stations in the United States who are not affiliated with any broadcast network. Several hundred others have part-time affiliations with one or more of the smaller networks (primarily UPN and WB). Most of these stations broadcast on the lower frequency, locally based UHF signal. Each one decides which programs to air throughout the broadcast day, and is responsible for selling its own commercial time.

Syndication

A major program source for independent stations is syndicated programming. Here, an individual program (or package of several programs) is sold on a station-by-station basis, regardless of that station's affiliation. It may be of any type or length. There are two main types—original shows and off-network fare. The former are filled with game shows, such as *Wheel of Fortune,* and talk shows such as *Oprah* or *Ellen*. They are sold either by the program's producers or by syndication companies, such as Viacom's King World, that put together packages of properties. The distinction between syndication and network shows is that syndicated programs can air at different times in different markets as well as on different networks. This leads to syndicated shows having to be "cleared" by each local station that chooses to buy them. The clearance figure refers to the percentage of markets across the country that can view that particular show. So, for example, if a syndicated talk show is "cleared" in 70% of the United States, it means that broadcast TV stations seen by 70% of all TV viewers have purchased that program. Syndication clearances generally range anywhere from 70% to 99%. It is worth noting, too, that some network programs do not have total (100%) clearance because an affiliate station may refuse to air them, or will put them on at a different time than the rest of the network. For example, NBC aired a mini-series featuring a priest who is less that perfect. Several of NBC's affiliate stations refused to air it, citing it as an "anti-Christian" program.[1]

The goal of many network programs is to produce enough episodes to go into the syndicated marketplace (usually 100 episodes). This is known as off-network programming, and helps fill up the hours of airtime that stations have when network shows aren't running. Programs that have been popular on the networks can continue to air for many years in syndication. Hits from the 1970s and 1980s, (e.g., *MASH*, *Cheers*, and *Cosby*) can still be seen on TV during the early evening or late night hours in syndication. Today, there are nearly 900 hours of syndicated programming produced each year for 148 different programs. The top ten programs in syndication appear in Exhibit 4.4.

Spot Television

Spot television is another way to purchase television time. Here, instead of contracting with the network to distribute a commercial to all of that network's affiliate stations across the country, an advertiser can pick and choose which programs and stations to use, placing the message in various "spots" across the country. As already noted, fewer than 100 of all TV stations are not affiliated with a network, and this number will continue to diminish as networks (and their multimedia conglomerate owners) buy up

---

[1]"More NBC Affiliates Drop 'Book of Daniel,'" Abbey Klaussen, AdAge.com, January 12, 2006.

Exhibit 4.4	Top 10 syndicated shows	
Rank	**Program**	**Rating**
1	Wheel of Fortune	9.0
2	Jeopardy!	7.1
3	Oprah Winfrey Show	7.6
4	Everybody Loves Raymond	6.9
5	Seinfeld	5.9
6	Friends	5.7
7	Seinfeld (Weekend)	5.5
8	CSI	5.5
9	Dr. Phil	5.2
10	Entertainment Tonight	5.2

Source: Broadcasting & Cable, 3/7/05

independents as regulation is relaxed on station ownership. The spot TV buy could be as small as a single station in one market, to a couple of hundred stations across a region. The actual cost of placing spots on local stations is lower than a total network buy, but it can become quite expensive once you start including a large number of markets.

Spot TV time is sold either by the individual station and/or by station representative firms, or *rep firms*. These firms put together packages of stations, known as *unwired networks* (because they are not physically linked together, or wired). Rep firms can usually customize buys for you, allowing you to pick only those stations that interest you in a given number of markets.

Cable Television

Cable television is sometimes thought of as a relatively new way to distribute programs and commercials, but in fact it has existed as a means of conveying television signals since 1948. Because it does not depend on over-the-air signals, but comes into the home via wires laid underground (or sometimes on poles on the street), reception is much clearer in many areas. That was the original reason behind its growth—so that people in Eugene, Oregon, or Lancaster, Pennsylvania could receive the signals of the broadcast networks more clearly. Whereas the broadcast networks distribute their programs from a central location to each of their affiliates, cable programs are sent via satellite from the cable network to individual cable operators (franchises) within each market, who then distribute the signals to the subscribers' homes. There are more than 10,000 separate cable systems operating today, although the majority belongs to one of the large multiple system operators (MSOs) that have cable systems in numerous markets. In 2004, the top three players were Comcast, Time Warner, and Cox. Together, these three operators serve 36% of all cable viewers in the country.

Another difference between broadcast TV and cable TV, from the consumers' standpoint, is that they must pay a monthly subscription fee to receive cable service. The average monthly cost of cable in 2005 was about $60. For an additional monthly fee, consumers can receive one or more of the pay cable networks, such as Home Box Office (HBO), Showtime, or The Disney Channel, which do not show any advertising at all.

Cable TV is made up of a wide variety of different networks, many of which specialize in certain kinds of programs or appeal to certain types of people. This was originally called *narrowcasting*, in contrast to the more diverse or broad-based programming found on broadcast TV. Cable News Network (CNN) shows 24 hours of news and information programming, whereas ESPN airs sports and Comedy Central has comedy. There are several cable networks, such as USA Network and TBS, which are more similar to the broadcast networks in their programming, airing a variety of different types of shows, from adventures to situation comedies to movies and dramas.

Exhibit 4.5 displays the biggest cable networks currently available, together with the number of subscribers to each one. The number of networks available varies by system. In recent years, most cable companies have spent large sums of money upgrading their physical plant to provide digital cable services that allow them to offer hundreds of different channels, rather than the 50–100 that were most common in the 1980s and 1990s. Exhibit 4.6 shows how the number of stations and channels available to viewers has increased over the past 15 years.

The development of cable TV as an advertising medium began in the early 1980s and has grown steadily ever since. Today, more than $21 billion of total TV advertising dollars go to cable television, representing nearly one third of the total amount advertisers spend in television. Most of cable's ad dollars are purchased on a national basis, although the medium has been growing rapidly at the local level as well. If you manage a local restaurant or a bank, you can run your commercials throughout the area, or you can confine your messages to a particular cable system's area. National advertisers can also use local cable, customizing their messages down to the neighborhood (system) level.

Through new technology companies, such as Visible World or Digeo, advertisers are starting to test *dynamic customization* of ads, allowing them to change their messages depending on the zipcode or time of day or program. For example, a credit card company could send one message to more affluent areas, talking about the benefits of its Platinum card, and another

EXHIBIT 4.5 Top 15 cable networks and subscribers

Rank	Network	Subscribers (000)
1	Discovery	89,900
2	ESPN	89,900
3	CNN (Cable News Network)	89,400
4	TNT (Turner Network Television)	89,400
5	USA Network	89,200
6	Nickelodeon	89,100
7	TBS (Superstation)	89,100
8	Spike TV	89,100
9	A&E Network	89,000
10	Lifetime Television	88,900
11	ESPN2	88,800
12	The Weather Channel	88,800
13	The Learning Channel	88,700
14	MTV	88,500
15	C-SPAN	88,400

Source: National Cable & Telecommunications Association, April 2005

EXHIBIT 4.6 Number of channels and stations received

Number of Stations	1-14	15-19	20-29	30+	Average number of stations per household
1985	78%	18%	4%	0%	11.0
1995	65%	25%	9%	1%	13.0
2004	50%	22%	24%	4%	16.4

Number of channels	1-14	15-19	20-29	30+	Average number of channels per household
1985	50%	15%	16%	19%	18.8
1995	17%	9%	6%	68%	41.1
2004	6%	4%	7%	83%	92.6

Source: Nielsen Media Research 2005

to more downscale areas, focusing more on the company's efforts to prevent identification theft. Ads for a fast food restaurant could be altered for each hour of the day that they appear, without having to create 24 different versions in advance. A computer database is created during commercial production that includes all the possible taglines, voiceovers, or footage required, and then the computer program works with the cable company's ad traffic system to send the right commercial to the right home at the right time.

Advertisers can also purchase time on several systems at once by going through a central sales office, known as an *interconnect*. This is similar to a rep firm—you select the cable systems on which your ad will appear. Most interconnects operate on a metropolitan or regional basis, such as Greater Chicago, or the Bay Area.

Satellite Television

Although listed here as a type of television, satellite TV is more of a means of distribution at this point. From being a way for rural inhabitants to receive any kind of signal via large C-band dishes, today's far smaller satellite dishes can be seen perched on the outside of houses all across the country, and are as common in urban markets as they are in rural or suburban areas. By delivering TV signals directly from the satellite and eliminating underground cables or those aboveground on poles, satellite services are able to offer a far larger number of channels to viewers. There are two major satellite providers: Dish Network and DirecTV network. About 22% of the country now receives television via satellite, and the battle between that form of distribution and cable is increasingly fierce. Without much of the high cost of transmission incurred by cable, satellite providers have been far quicker to offer new or high technology services to customers, including two-way interaction with the TV set and the functionality of digital video recorders (see next section).

NEW FORMS OF TELEVISION

The development of new forms of television began in the early 1990s, but it was not until the latter part of that decade that technology began to catch up with the pipe dreams of the inventors. One of the first to be available was *pay-per-view* (PPV). Here, several channels are allocated to special programs, such as movies or sporting events, purchased by the cable subscriber on an individual basis. They may cost as little as a few dollars or as much as $100 (e.g., for a special boxing match). In order to be able to receive this form of programming, the cable linking the television to the cable system operator must be two-way, or *addressable,* allowing the operator to deliver the program to individual households on demand. At present, more than half of all homes are addressable.

An extension of PPV is video on demand (VOD). This allows viewers to order up any program that they want to watch, at any time. Although its availability has become quite widespread (about 35% of all homes), the number of people using it remains fairly small, in large part due to the lack of "content," or programming, that people want to buy. It is something of a chicken-and-egg situation. Programmers or cable operators do not want to invest heavily to create programs if there are not enough people willing to pay for it, but people will not want to buy it until there is a sufficient variety of good programs available.

VOD's expansion has occurred largely due to the growth of digital cable, which is now in about 20 million homes. All of the major cable system operators have been rapidly upgrading their systems in recent years, seeing great potential in enhancing their revenues not only by offering more channels to viewers, but also by selling numerous ancillary services, from Internet access through the TV set to special channels featuring local news and weather. With some of these enhancements, for example, viewers can call up sports statistics as an overlay on the screen while viewing a football or baseball game.

Another way that television is being altered is through the video recorder. The introduction of digital video recorders (DVRs) at the tail end of the 1990s promised to revolutionize the way people watched TV and, as a result, the advertising business for that medium. Although its growth has been relatively slow, with about 7% of U.S. homes owning recorders at the end of 2005, the concept and technology do, indeed, suggest a radically new way to view television. DVRs, offered by companies such as TiVo and cable companies like Comcast and Time Warner, put a large computer hard drive onto the video recorder that allows it to digitize the program as it is delivered to the TV set and, therefore, give consumers the ability to fast-forward or pause programs as they air and to skip commercials. At the same time, viewers can program the device to find programs to record on a regular basis either by title (all new episodes of "Law and Order," e.g.) or by actor/director (e.g., find me anything with Brad Pitt). As a result, the official program schedule evaporates, and consumers become their own program scheduler, watching whatever programs they want, whenever they choose.

The implications for advertising are potentially huge. As discussed in chapter 6, television is planned to a large extent based on program dayparts. What happens when there is no such thing as "prime-time" television anymore? And what if the viewership of a program no longer occurs simultaneously because large numbers of people are recording the program for viewing at a later date? What would the program rating be based on? Last but not least, these DVR devices make it easy to fast-forward or skip commercials, something that the manufacturers have realized is a double-edged sword, because the possible absence of ads will cut off an important revenue source for networks and programmers alike. One analysis by Accenture estimated the lost revenue to television due to DVRs and VOD will be a mammoth $27 billion by 2009.[2]

The use of the TV to connect to the Internet, and the computer to view television, has been happening slowly. Despite promises that the two devices would become interchangeable by the 21st century, consumers have shown that they see them each as distinct and different from the other. TV viewing tends to be a more passive, "lean back" experience, in contrast to the active involvement required of the "lean forward" computer/Internet activity. Nevertheless, we are likely to continue to see new attempts to somehow merge the two media in the future, with more Internet functions (e.g., searching or pop-up ads) appearing on the TV screen, and more TV offerings (programs and TV commercials) migrating to the small screen.[3] For example, in 2005, Pepsi announced that its Pepsi Smash TV show would move from the WB broadcast network to Yahoo Music. This followed the premiere airing of a Showtime pay cable network series, *Fat Actress*, which appeared first on Yahoo in March 2005.[4] It is also worth noting that both Google and Yahoo!, two key web-focused companies, are developing the technology to allow for consumer searching on TV similar to the way consumers already conduct Internet searches (see p. 91 for more on search).

Another significant shift in the use of television has been taking place on the advertising side with the growth and development of *brand integration* (i.e., product placement). Here, advertisers pay the program producer to put their brands into the storylines or content of TV shows. Sometimes this is done overtly, like the challenges on *The Apprentice* to sell products like Dove soap or create a marketing campaign for Pontiac's G6. It was estimated that, in 2005, advertisers would spend $4.25 billion to place their brands within TV shows. This is more than three times the amount they were spending 6 years earlier ($1.63 billion). The difference between integration and placement is that, in the latter, the product appears more or less as a "prop," such as a character being seen to open a box of General Mills' Wheaties cereal rather than Brand X. Now, those companies that make cleaning products like Clorox pay to appear in Lifetime network's "How Clean Is Your House?" and fashion companies pay to have their brands given away on Bravo's *Queer Eye for the Straight Guy*.[5]

---

[2]"DVRs: A $27B Revenue Killer," Claire Atkinson, *Advertising Age,* April 18, 2005, 45.

[3]"Cross Media Promotion of the Internet in Television Commercials," Steven Edwards and Carrie La Ferle, *Journal of Current Issues and Research in Advertising,* vol. 22, no. 1, Spring 2000, 1–12.

[4]"'Pepsi Smash' TV Show Moves to Yahoo," Kate MacArthur, Ad Age.com, June 3, 2005.

[5]"Sharing the Spotlight," Daisy Whitney, *New York Times,* May 10, 2005, ZX11.

One of the more prominent efforts at paid product integration occurred in September 2004, when GM gave away its newly launched Pontiac G6 vehicles to every member of the studio audience in Oprah Winfrey's daytime talk show. In keeping with the theme of the program, to fulfill people's "wildest dreams," Oprah gave away 276 vehicles, each of which had an estimated value of $28,400. The event generated enormous publicity for the company, most of it favorable, and Pontiac registered a record number of visits to its Web site in the days following the show.[6] In another case, Burger King paid between $2 million and $3.5 million to appear in the hit TV show, *The Apprentice*, with the contestants charged to run a franchise restaurant in New York while a new sandwich was being launched. That allowed viewers to see how the restaurant really worked, and to get lots of exposure to the new product. In the weeks following the airing of the episode, sales of that sandwich rose to 1.2 million, 20% higher than expected. At the same time, the promotion was featured on the BK Web site, generating 600,000 visits to find out more and enter a sweepstakes.[7]

BENEFITS OF TELEVISION TO ADVERTISERS

Whichever type of television advertising you choose, you will enjoy a number of benefits unavailable from any other media. Among these benefits, television's ability to imitate real-life situations, its pervasiveness, and its broad reach are most noteworthy.

True to Life

The most obvious advantage of television advertising is the opportunity to use *sight, sound, color,* and *motion* in commercials. This form of advertising is generally considered the most lifelike, recreating scenes and showing people in situations with which we can all identify. That does not mean we don't see cartoons or animated commercials, or fantasies on the screen; today's electronic wizardry lets TV ads show us everything imaginable. But of all the media available, TV comes closest to showing us products in our everyday lives. This is not only important for package goods advertisers (i.e., firms such as Pillsbury, Anheuser-Busch, or Unilever, who are able to show us what their products look like and how they are used or enjoyed) but also for service companies such as Marriott Hotels or American Express, which can offer us ways to use their amenities. As the Internet continues to expand, and bandwidth grows, more TV-like ads have appeared there too. Ameri-

---

[6]"Pontiac Gets Major Mileage Out of $8 Million 'Oprah' deal," Jean Halliday and Claire Atkinson, *Advertising Age*, September 20, 2004, 12.

[7]"Burger King Cooks Up a Winner: Best Overall," Amy Johannes, Promo Magazine Web site, May 3, 2005.

can Express was one of the first advertisers to launch a TV ad (starring comedian Jerry Seinfeld) on the Internet before it appeared on television.

The Most Pervasive Medium

Television advertising is the most pervasive media form available. Several slogans from TV commercials have entered the mainstream of conversation, such as Bud Light's "Whassup?", or Wisk detergent's infamous "ring around the collar" line. Characters in commercials have also become part of our lives, such as the lonely Maytag repairman or Tony the Tiger for Kellogg's Frosted Flakes.

Reaching the Masses

Another important advantage of television from an advertising perspective is the wide *reach* of people it offers at any one time. Even in programs with ratings of 8 or 10, you are reaching about 9 million individuals! There is generally a slightly smaller audience for the commercials than for the programs themselves, nevertheless, television remains a truly mass medium. Moreover, by buying time on several different programs shown at different times and/or on different days, it is possible to reach a wide *variety* of individuals. An individual ad appears for a short time (usually 15 or 30 seconds), but if it is repeated on several occasions more people are likely to be exposed to it, often more than once. This helps build brand awareness, which in turn may lead to the formation of favorable attitudes or intentions to purchase that brand.

DRAWBACKS OF TELEVISION ADVERTISING

Unfortunately, television advertising has unique drawbacks as well as the unique benefits just discussed. Four of the most commonly encountered drawbacks are cost, limited exposure time, cluttered airwaves, and poor placement of ads within or between programs.

Dollars and Sense

Perhaps the biggest disadvantage for advertising on TV, particularly at the national level, is the high cost. The average 30-second network commercial during prime time in 2005 cost $200,000. An ad in the 2005 Super Bowl, television's most expensive ad opportunity, cost about $2.6 million. For many advertisers, this is way beyond their budget, leading them to cable or spot TV as cheaper alternatives.

Quick Cuts

Another drawback to this medium is its brief exposure time. Although many ads are seen several times within a short period of time, unless the commercial is particularly inventive or unusual it is likely the viewer will ignore it or be irritated by seeing it after the first few occasions and deliberately try to avoid the message.[8] Controversy remains over just how many times people can be exposed to spots without getting bored or annoyed, a phenomenon referred to as commercial *wearout*. In the future, this drawback may be avoided through *interactive TV*, where viewers select the kinds of messages they are more interested in, finding out more about a specific brand or product in detail. The key here is that this self-selected audience is more interested and involved in the message.

Cluttering the Airwaves

A related factor that is becoming an increasing concern for advertisers is the sheer number of ads appearing on TV as seen in Exhibit 4.7. This leads to clutter of spots, again believed to reduce the effectiveness of individual commercials.[9] There is evidence to support this fear. From 1990 to 2000, there was a 31% increase in the number of spots shown on prime-time network TV. Part of the explanation for this is the increase in the number of broadcast networks (FOX, UPN, WB, PAX). But another major reason is the growth in the number of shorter length commercials. For many years, the standard television spot lasted a full minute. Then, in the mid-1960s more advertisers started using 30-second commercials and found them to be more cost-efficient and no less effective. As costs continued to increase during the 1970s and early 1980s, advertisers tried the same tactic, shifting to even smaller

EXHIBIT 4.7   Commercial clutter trend: prime time

	Number	Percent Change (Yr on Yr)
1990	2,059	
1995	3,177	35.2%
2000	4,751	33.1%
2004	5,264	9.7%

Source: Nielsen Media Research 2005

---

[8]"Predictors of Advertising Avoidance in Print and Broadcast Media," Paul Surgi Speck and Michael T. Elliott, *Journal of Advertising*, vol. 26, no. 2, Summer 1997, 61–76.

[9]"Does Advertising Clutter Have Diminishing and Negative Returns?" Louisa Ha and Barry R. Litman, *Journal of Advertising*, vol. 26, no. 1, Spring 1997, 31–42.

commercial lengths. Today, the 15-second spot accounts for 37% of all prime-time network TV commercials. The result of clutter on consumers is questionable, but research suggests that it hinders the communication, sometimes considerably.[10]

Placing Spots

Another area that has provoked a good deal of discussion is where commercials should be placed for optimal effectiveness. For network TV, you can buy time either within the program (*in-program*) or between two shows (*break*). Whereas some believe there is no difference in viewer attention between these two options, others feel that you are likely to lose more viewers during the breaks than within the program itself. On spot TV, the break position used to be the only timeslot available, although in recent years the "rules" have been relaxed. Commercial breaks have slid a few minutes into the program rather than appearing only at the top or bottom of each hour.

Related to this issue is where to position your commercial within the series, or *pod*, of spots being shown. Evidence suggests that the first ad to appear will receive the most attention, followed by the last one; those in the middle are likely to suffer from viewers switching channels, not looking at the screen, or leaving the room. Advertisers, however, do not routinely get the choice of where in the pod to air their ad. Some advertisers will pay a premium to ensure their ad appears first, but this is not always permitted.

EXHIBIT 4.8	Growth of 15-second commercials in prime time		
	1990	**1995**	**2000**	**2004**
:15	44%	44%	48%	37%
:30	51%	55%	46%	59%
:60	<1%	<1%	3%	3%
Other	5%	1%	2%	1%
	100%	100%	100%	100%

Source: Nielsen Media Research 2005

---

[10]"Consumer Perceptions of Advertising Clutter and Its Impact Across Various Media," Michael T. Elliott and Paul Surgi Speck, *Journal of Advertising Research*, vol. 35, no. 3, May/June 1995, 29–42. "The Antecedents and Consequences of Perceived Advertising Clutter," Paul Surgi Speck and Michael T. Elliott, *Journal of Current Issues and Research in Advertising*, vol. 19, no. 2, 1997, 39–54.

RESEARCH ON TELEVISION

Much of the research literature on television has focused on two key issues: the impact of a lifelike message and the effects of program environment. Buchholz and Smith found that the more "involved" consumers are in the medium, the stronger their cognitive responses to ad messages.[11] Kamins et al. examined how TV ads are evaluated depending on the mood created by the program in which the ads appear.[12] There are many other research articles as well.[13]

RADIO—THE "EVERYWHERE" MEDIUM

Radio is the oldest electronic advertising medium. It first became popular in America in the early 1920s and since that time has managed to hold its own against all other media forms. Although families no longer sit around their radios as they once did to listen to the most popular programs of the day, they still rely on this medium for both information and entertainment. Indeed, almost every home in America has at least one radio, and most have several. People listen to the radio, on average, for 3 hours 17 minutes every day, and the medium reaches 73% of everyone age 12 and older each day (94% each week). Most listening (84%) occurs between 6 a.m. and 10 a.m. Increasingly, that listening occurs outside of the home. Almost all cars (95%) are fitted with radios now, and people can carry the medium with them wherever they go. Nearly half (44%) of radio listening occurs in the car, and 37% happens at home and 19% is at work or elsewhere.

---

[11]"The Role of Consumer Involvement in Determining Cognitive Response to Broadcast Advertising," Laura M. Buchholz and Robert E. Smith, *Journal of Advertising*, vol. 20, no. 1, 1991, 4–17.

[12]"Television Commercial Evaluation in the Context of Program Induced Mood: Congruency Versus Consistency Effects," Michael A. Kamins, Lawrence J. Marks, and Deborah Skinner, *Journal of Advertising*, vol. 20, no. 2, June 1991, 1–14.

[13]"Multiple Resource Theory and Consumer Processing of Broadcast Advertisements: An Involvement Perspective," Robert E. Smith and Laura M. Buchholz, *Journal of Advertising*, vol. 20, no. 3, September 1991, 1–8. "Attention Versus Distraction: The Interactive Effect of Program Involvement and Attentional Devices on Commercial Processing," Kenneth R. Lord and Robert E. Burnkrant, *Journal of Advertising*, vol. 22, no. 1, March 1993, 47–60. "Television Programming and Its Influence on Viewers' Perceptions of Commercials: The Role of Program Arousal and Pleasantness," V. Carter Broach, Jr., Thomas R. Page, Jr., and R. Dale Wilson, *Journal of Advertising*, vol. 24, no. 4, Winter 1995, 45–54. "Context Is Key: The Effect of Program-Induced Mood on Thoughts About the Ad," Andrew B. Aylesworth and Scott B. MacKenzie, *Journal of Advertising*, vol. 27, no. 2, Summer 1998, 17–32. "Hearing Versus Seeing: A Comparison of Consumer Learning of Spoken and Pictorial Information in Television Advertising," Wendy J. Bryce and Richard F. Yalch, *Journal of Current Issues and Research in Advertising*, vol. 15, no. 1, Spring 1993, 1–20. "Program Involvement: Are Moderate Levels Best for Ad Memory and Attitude Toward the Ad?" Nader T. Tavassoli, Clifford J. Shultz II, and Gavan J. Fitzsimons, *Journal of Advertising Research*, vol. 35, no. 5, September/October 1995, 61–72.

There are nearly 14,000 radio stations across the country. Of those, 4,975 operate on the AM (amplitude modulation) wavelength, and 8,863 are FM (frequency modulation) stations. The primary differences between them are in reception area and audience. AM stations can broadcast over a wider distance, but because the soundwaves are impeded by any kind of obstruction (hills, tall buildings) the sound quality is inferior to FM stations, which broadcast in a narrower listening area. Older adults listen to more AM radio, reflecting the fact that more AM stations offer news and talk programs. FM radio is dominated by music formats, which attract younger listeners. Radio stations are either commercial, accepting advertising as their chief source of revenue, or noncommercial, funded by public monies and/or audience sponsorships. Commercial stations, on average, will air anywhere from 9 to 20 ads per hour, frequently concentrated in blocks of 3 minutes or more.

As with television, radio is classified by both daypart and format. The different formats that are available for the advertiser are not defined the same way by the listener. Radio dayparts and formats are shown in Exhibits 4.9 and 4.10.

EXHIBIT 4.9   Radio formats

Adult Contemporary

Adult Standards

Alternative

Contemporary Hit Radio

Classical

Country

New AC/Smooth Talk/Jazz

News/Talk/Information

Oldies

Religious

Rock

Spanish

Urban

EXHIBIT 4.10   Radio networks

ABC

Premiere

Westwood One

American Urban

Today, radio represents a little over 7% of all advertising expenditures. The two main types of radio advertising are network (national) and spot (local). The way programs and ads are distributed is similar to that of network and spot broadcast TV.

Network Radio

Unlike television, network radio is less important to advertisers than is local radio. It currently receives about 4% of all radio dollars. Like TV, however, a message placed on network radio is distributed via satellite to each network's affiliate stations. These stations are paid an annual sum to take, or "clear," the network's programs. Perhaps surprisingly, almost two thirds of all radio stations are affiliated with a network. The kinds of programs they receive from the network may be aired every day, such as the ABC newscast, or periodically, such as Casey Kasem's Weekly Top 40 show. There are presently four major radio networks, each of which has subdivisions based on the programming and the demographic makeup of their listeners. Altogether, there are 47 different networks. Westwood CBS News Primetime is aimed primarily at listeners from 25 to 54 years old through news radio. The stations that are part of ABC Young Adult Radio tend to be favored by younger adults, under age 35, with contemporary hit radio and urban formats. Exhibit 4.11 lists the top 10 networks.

From an advertiser's perspective, one key benefit of using network radio is that you can go through a single source to place your ads across a region or across the country. The downside of this form of radio, however, is that

EXHIBIT 4.11　Top 10 radio networks

Rank	Network	Audience (000)
1	ABC Daytime Direction	7,420
2	Westwood CBS News Primetime	5,980
3	Premiere Morning Drive	5,437
4	Jones MediaAmerica TWC Radio	5,318
5	ABC Morning News Radio	5,268
6	Dial-Global Complete FM	4,477
7	Premiere Mediabase	4,003
8	ABC News/Talk Radio	3,945
9	Premiere Emerald Plus	3,942
10	ABC Young Adult Radio	3,556

Note: Data are for Monday-Sunday, 6A-12 Midnight, Persons 12+
Source: Arbitron's RADAR 84, March 2005

you have less flexibility in choosing the stations you wish to be in. If you buy the CBS Spectrum Radio Network, you may get the number one station in Biloxi, Mississippi, but the fourth place station in Little Rock, Arkansas.

Spot Radio

About 96% of radio's advertising dollars are spent in spot markets, where you buy time on individual stations on a market-by-market basis. Here, if you were placing the advertising for Coldwell Banker realtors, you could buy time on individual stations in a market, regardless of which network they belong to, and choose which markets to target. The advantage of purchasing radio in this way is that you can select the exact stations and/or markets in which you wish to advertise your product. This also allows you to customize the message to each location so that Home Depot home improvement stores, for example, can mention the address or phone number of different locations in each market's ad.

Some stations are linked together only for the purpose of selling advertising time. They constitute an "unwired" network, allowing you to select which stations within the group you wish to use based on your demographic or geographic preferences. Typically, an advertiser buys time through a representative, or rep firm, rather than dealing with every station individually. So if you are trying to target teens with the Sony PSP videogame, then you could go to a rep firm that offers you stations that do well against that group. Examples of unwired networks include the Wall Street Journal Radio Network, which offers classical music and performs well against adults over age 25. Again, for the advertiser, using a network of this kind provides you with a single invoice for all of the stations. But, as with wired network radio, you may end up buying time on less attractive stations as part of the package deal.

Satellite Radio

In 2001, satellite radio services were introduced to the U.S. marketplace. XM Radio and Sirius Radio both deliver about 100 different channels via national satellites. Consumers need special receivers in order to tune in to these services, and they must pay a monthly subscription (about $10–$15/month) for the privilege. There is one incentive to pay because about half of the stations air without commercials. XM has 71 channels of music and 29 entertainment/news/sports offerings. One third of the total is without commercials. Sirius has 50 commercial-free music channels and 50 with other content. Even on those channels that include advertising, the amount will be far less than on regular radio stations—6 minutes per hour, as compared to 15–20 minutes on terrestrial stations.

The content offered by satellite radio ranges from niche forms of music to college radio stations that let alumni keep up with their favorite college sports teams to syndicated talk show hosts (e.g., Howard Stern or Rush Limbaugh). This type of radio resembles cable TV in that there are so many channels, they can afford to be highly specialized (e.g., a Nascar channel, several baseball channels, or a channel offering bluegrass music). Both satellite radio companies have deals with the major U.S. auto manufacturers, who have built satellite radio capability into more of their models and are offering it as a standard piece of equipment in their luxury vehicles. As of mid-2005, about 4 million homes had satellite radio service. The jury remains out, however, as to whether consumers will be willing to pay for something they are used to getting for free. Although people "learned" to pay for television back in the 1980s, the perceived value of the radio medium among most radio listeners may not be as high.

Streaming Audio

As the Internet develops further, more people are listening to the radio via their computers through a technology generally known as streaming audio. Radio signals are digitized, and then sent through the Internet. Many traditional, land-based stations offer simultaneous signals on the Web, whereas other stations have been created solely online. While still accounting for a small proportion of total listening, surveys suggest that nearly one third (34%) of the population has at some point tuned in to radio on the Web, with 8% having claimed to do so in the past week.

BENEFITS OF RADIO TO ADVERTISERS

As an advertiser, you cannot afford to ignore the many benefits of radio advertising. Although it does not offer the visual power of television advertising, it does provide the opportunity to reach targeted audiences frequently, at a reasonable cost. These and other benefits of this medium are discussed below.

Local Appeal

As mentioned earlier, most advertising dollars in radio are spent at the local or regional level rather than on the networks. Radio is therefore listened to primarily as a local medium, allowing people the opportunity to tie in to local events, news, or celebrities.

Reaching the Right Audience

Because of the way radio stations are formatted, the medium provides you with targeted, specific audiences. If you run a local health club, then you can reach women from age 25 to 54 by placing your message on light rock stations. Or, as the owner of a religious bookstore, you can promote your store by advertising on the local religious radio station. Radio also offers good opportunities for reaching ethnic groups. In areas with sizable Black or Hispanic populations, you are likely to find at least one station that appeals to each of these minorities. It will generally have a very loyal following. For a baby clothing manufacturer, for example, advertising to Hispanics may turn out to be very profitable because they tend to have larger families than non-Hispanic households. And, in 2005, radio audience measurement company Arbitron released its first-ever survey results of Chinese listeners in both New York and Los Angeles. The results showed that 56% of all listening done by these consumers was to Chinese language radio.

Imagery Transfer

For many advertisers, radio is seen as a secondary medium, used in conjunction with a major print or television campaign. The good news here is that research has shown the power of radio ads to create a visual image in listeners' minds from the TV commercials they have seen for that same brand.[14] This process, known as *imagery transfer*, gives radio ads far more impact than the auditory stimulus alone and, therefore, greater potential influence on consumer response.

Keeping Costs Down

Compared with television, radio is an extremely inexpensive ad medium. A 30-second spot in prime time on a broadcast TV network may run as high as $500,000, whereas the price for that same length commercial on a local radio station will be closer to $11,000. Of course, these costs are linked to the number of people you will be reaching.

Building Frequency

With a TV buy, you are usually looking for high reach numbers. In order to gain frequency, you need either a very large budget or inexpensive dayparts. On radio, however, because the costs are so low, it makes sense to buy a lot of time and build up frequency against your target audience. It also makes sense to do this for strategic reasons; people tend to listen to a particular station for a fairly brief period of time, so you want to ensure you reach them while they are listening. You should keep in mind that listening habits are not seasonal, so frequency can be built up year-round.

---

[14]Imagery Transfer Study conducted by Statistical Research, Inc., 1999.

Radio and Purchasing

Research shows that the time between media exposure and purchase is shorter for radio than for any other traditional medium, as shown in Exhibit 4.12. This means that your potential consumers may well be listening while they are making their purchase decisions.

A 2005 study undertaken by the Radio Advertising Effectiveness Lab (RAEL) on behalf of the Radio Advertising Bureau found that in a controlled test, consumers exposed to radio ads along with TV were more likely to buy the advertised product than those who were only exposed to an equivalent amount of TV ads.[15]

Flexible Messages

Compared to the high production costs and long lead times of television, radio is extremely flexible. If your ad is read live on the air, as is often done, you can change the message at very short notice without much difficulty. You can vary the message for different dayparts or station formats, perhaps using different music backgrounds depending on the type of music played on that station. Radio also offers the flexibility of tie-ins to local retailers or other promotional opportunities, such as local contests or events.

EXHIBIT 4.12   Time Between Media Exposure and Purchase

	Percent exposed to medium within an hour of purchase
Radio	59%
Outdoor	27%
TV	20%
Magazines	11%
Newspapers	10%

Source: Radio Advertising Bureau, 2001

---

[15]Radio Advertising Effectiveness Lab (RAEL) studies, as reported in *2004–2005 Radio Marketing Guide & Fact Book*, produced by the Radio Advertising Bureau, New York.

DRAWBACKS OF RADIO ADVERTISING

In addition to the numerous benefits of radio advertising, there are a few drawbacks to keep in mind as well. Each of these can be seen as a challenge; most can be overcome with some planning and creativity.

In the Background

When we listen to the radio, we are usually doing something else at the same time, making it a background medium. Ads on radio must therefore work a lot harder to grab—and keep—our attention.

Sound Only

Radio can only offer sound, rather than the sight and motion of television. However, the medium can still be used to great effect because it offers the possibility of inspiring the listener's imagination. They can hear the waves crashing against rocks, or breaking glass, or party chatter, and conjure up images in their mind of what the scene looks like. Radio advertisements also tend to feature humor fairly often both as a way to get attention and because the audience is less likely to be distracted by any visuals and can listen to the words. And as already noted, if used in conjunction with similar TV commercials, listeners will often transfer the TV images to the radio spot.

Short Message Life

Because people have the radio on in the background, for the most part, ads on this medium have a very short message life. Radio is like TV, and unlike newspapers and magazines, because once the ad has aired, the opportunity for exposure has disappeared. This makes it all the more critical to grab the audience's attention right away with a message that is relevant, involving, and interesting.

Fragmentation

One of the drawbacks for radio is the fragmentation of the medium. We no longer just have "rock" stations, but "active rock," "classic rock," and "album-oriented rock" formats, among others. Each one appeals to slightly different kinds of people, so if you wanted to reach them all, you would have to buy each type of rock station in a market. Audience shares, particularly in major markets, may be very small, which makes it hard to use the medium as a reach vehicle.

RESEARCH ON RADIO

Although radio is considered a "second cousin" to television in the realm of electronic ad media, research has been done to compare the two forms. In addition, the power of sound, and of music in particular, has been studied to see how that impacts radio ad effectiveness. Legal issues in the radio business are noted here, because the legal policies adopted by radio stations as far as which ads are accepted have a direct impact on the kinds of radio commercials that are broadcast.[16]

In 2003, the radio industry started to fund significant research studies under the umbrella of the Radio Advertising Effectiveness Lab (RAEL). This consortium of advertisers, agencies, and radio station groups helped fund and design several major studies that examined the impact of radio advertising on consumers. Its first work looked at radio's psychological role in consumers' lives. Its study, "Personal Relevance, Personal Connections," found that radio listening is considered by people to be a personal and emotion-driven experience. They listen for personal gratification more so than for entertainment or pure information. As noted earlier in this section, another study looked at the benefits of synergistically mixing radio ads with newspaper or TV ads. It exposed consumers to two radio ads or one TV plus two radio ads, and did the same substituting newspaper for TV. What they found was radio ads alone performed better than either the single exposure to TV or newspapers (in terms of brand recall). When radio was used together with TV, brand awareness and brand recall were higher than either medium alone.[17]

ALL THE NEWS THAT'S FIT TO PRINT—NEWSPAPER ADVERTISING

Newspapers are one of the oldest media forms in this country. They were also one of the earliest media to accept advertising. In fact, the first advertising agencies were established to handle the purchase of space in newspapers. Some of the earliest ads were for "medicinal" remedies, such as Lydia Pinkham's Compound.

---

[16]"Information Processing Differences Among Broadcast Media: Review and Suggestions for Research," James H. Leigh, *Journal of Advertising*, vol. 20, no. 2, June 1991, 71–76. "Mental Imagery and Sound Effects in Radio Commercials," Darryl W. Miller and Lawrence J. Marks, *Journal of Advertising*, vol, 21, no. 4, December 1992, 83–94. "Advertising Clearance Practices of Radio Stations: A Model of Advertising Self-Regulation," Avery M. Abernethy, *Journal of Advertising*, vol. 22, no. 3, September 1993, 15–26. "Creating the Contrast: The Influence of Silence and Background Music on Recall and Attribute Importance," G. Douglas Olsen, *Journal of Advertising*, vol. 24, no. 4, Winter 1995, 29–44.

[17]Radio Advertising Effectiveness Lab (RAEL) studies, as reported in *2004–2005 Radio Marketing Guide & Fact Book*, produced by the Radio Advertising Bureau, New York.

In contrast to many other countries with national newspapers, the majority of U.S. newspapers are written for and distributed to a primarily local audience. As a result, most advertising is placed on a market-by-market basis. You can also choose which section of the paper to appear in, such as news (local, national, or international), sports, entertainment, business, fashion, food, home, and travel, among others.

There are currently 2,373 newspapers published in the United States. This figure includes both weekday and Sunday editions (1,456 and 917, respectively). That number has remained relatively stable over time. In 1970, for example, there were 2,334 papers published. Newspaper audiences are measured in terms of *circulation*, or the number of people who subscribe to or purchase the newspaper. Exhibit 4.13 shows the top 10 papers across the country based on their circulation.

The past decade has witnessed a decline in the percentage of the adult population that admits to reading a paper daily. Currently, about 54% claim they do so, in contrast to the 78% who read a paper back in 1970. What is even more worrisome for the newspaper industry is that the readership figure is lower among younger people, who constitute the medium's future readers. Several papers have introduced daily low-priced tabloid papers to entice younger people to develop a newspaper reading habit. The *Chicago Tribune*'s Red Eye, for example, sells about 90,000 copies of its daily tabloid, primarily to readers under age 40, at the low per-issue cost of $0.25.

Another problem the industry faces is the demise of the two-newspaper town. Most large cities used to have at least two competing newspapers; today, due to the high costs of running a newspaper, that is the exception

EXHIBIT 4.13   Top 10 newspapers by circulation

Rank	Newspaper	Circulation (000)
1	USA Today	2220.9
2	Wall Street Journal	2106.8
3	New York Times	1121.1
4	Los Angeles Times	902.2
5	New York Daily News	715.1
6	Washington Post	707.7
7	New York Post	686.2
8	Chicago Tribune	599.5
9	Houston Chronicle	554.8
10	San Francisco Chronicle	480.6

Source: Audit Bureau of Circulations, as reported in Ad Age, 11/8/04, 16

rather than the rule. Only the largest cities (New York, Los Angeles, Chicago) still support two or three daily papers. This not only harms the newspaper industry, it is not particularly good news for advertisers either. Without competition, the paper can set its advertising rates wherever it wants them, as long as it can still compete with other media alternatives.

As major cities have dropped competing papers, some of the readership has moved to suburban or weekly newspapers. The growth here is not too surprising, given population shifts from city to suburb in the past few decades. The focus of these titles is far more local, writing about high school sports scores or local ordinances rather than national or regional news. For advertisers, it offers the opportunity to bring the message down to the truly local level. National advertisers such as Gap Stores can announce the opening of a new store in Arlington Heights, Illinois, in the *Arlington Heights Post*, instead of a zoned or regional edition of the *Chicago Tribune*.

Newspaper Advertising Revenue

The largest part of newspaper advertising revenue (45%) comes from retailers. This includes large companies, such as major national department stores like JC Penney and Nordstrom, to regional banks like National City or First National, down to Joe's shoe repair shop around the corner. Second in importance as far as newspaper ad revenues are concerned is classified advertising (40%). The most important classified sections are for real estate and automotive, which together account for the majority of classified ad dollars.

The third type of newspaper advertising is placed on a national basis so that it appears in all (or most) papers across the country. This type represents only 15% of total advertising revenues for the medium, despite the efforts of many newspapers to position themselves as valuable national vehicles in the face of increased competition with other local media, such as spot TV and radio, regional magazines, or billboards. The main problem that advertisers have with using newspapers on a national basis is the considerable premium that it costs to run their ads in all markets. Most are reluctant to pay that premium, which can cost up to 75% more than a local or regional ad.[18]

Newspapers also offer a medium within a medium, in the form of *free-standing inserts* (FSIs). These are pre-printed sheets that are usually distributed within the Sunday paper. Most carry coupons. On Sunday, too, most newspapers carry a special magazine supplement, either produced by the paper itself or coming from one of the nationally syndicated Sunday supplements (i.e., *Parade* and *USA Weekend*).

---

[18]"A Study of National Advertising's Payout: Image Ads in Newspaper ROP," Stuart Tolley, *Journal of Advertising Research*, vol. 33, no. 5, September/October 1993, 11–20.

At one point, it seemed that newspaper classified advertising would be greatly diminished by the Internet. Automotive and real estate classified ad sites were very popular at first and threatened to take revenues from the printed newspapers. It did not take long for newspapers to set up their own Internet-based advertising sites, either as part of their own individual newspaper sites (e.g., bostonglobe.com) or in concert with other newspapers (e.g., careercentral.com). Today, about 1,500 North American newspapers have Web sites, as do 5,000 papers globally. Increasingly, however, the newspapers' readers are migrating online instead of picking up the printed copy. Nielsen NetRatings calculates that about one in five (21%) of online users who read newspapers are reading them on the Web.

One issue that newspaper advertisers are increasingly trying to deal with is the "sacred" line between the advertising and editorial departments. General Motors, for example, pulled its advertising from the *Los Angeles Times* newspaper after a journalist for the paper wrote a critical review about the automaker's new Pontiac G6 vehicle. GM claimed there were mistakes in the article.[19] This may be the start of a trend, with major advertisers attempting to put clauses in their contracts that overtly state they will pull their ads if unfavorable editorial content appears. This is a slippery slope, potentially leading to a blurring of the church and state separation of editorial and advertising departments.

BENEFITS OF NEWSPAPERS TO ADVERTISERS

As Exhibit 4.13 illustrated, the top 10 U.S. newspapers reach about 10 million consumers every day. Add to that the circulations of the other, smaller, newspapers in the country, and you'll begin to see just what kind of exposure is possible with newspaper advertisements. But, in addition to reach, newspapers offer advertisers a number of important benefits that are discussed below.

Timeliness

The day after the stock market crashed in 1987, ads appeared in many newspapers reassuring consumers and stockholders that everything was still all right. Financial services companies reacted similarly after the terrorist attack on the World Trade Center in 2001. And McDonald's quickly responded in newspaper ads when it discovered that someone at one of its agencies had stolen winning game cards to several of its "instant-win" promotions. The company immediately created newspaper and TV ads to

---

[19]"Advertising," Stuart Elliott, *New York Times*, April 7, 2005, p. C3.

apologize to the public, and then added a new game with daily prizes awarded randomly to customers in the store.[20]

Unlike magazines or even television, newspapers are by their very nature filled with "news." People turn to them for the latest information on products, prices, and availability. The role that newspaper advertisements play in purchase decisions may be critical. A survey found that 70% of all newspaper readers agreed with the following statement: "The paper helps me to decide where to shop and buy." And 65% felt that the newspaper was more important than television in making purchase decisions. In addition, electronic scanner devices in most supermarkets and retail stores are now able to assess the link between advertising and sales more directly and rapidly. Data suggest that newspaper ads can triple the sales volume for items that are advertised at reduced prices.

Desirable Audience

In the battle to attract advertisers, newspapers can offer highly desirable audiences. A newspaper reader is more likely to be better educated, have a higher income, and be more involved in upscale activities than nonreaders. People with a household income of $75,000 a year or more are more likely to be newspaper readers. Exhibit 4.14 gives a profile of the newspaper audience.

In contrast to other media, readers spend a considerable amount of time with the newspaper, although that varies by age. Older readers (age 65+) spend about 1 hour a day with the paper, whereas the youngest adults (age 20–29) read daily for only 20 minutes[21] (most likely because they are going

---

EXHIBIT 4.14   Profile of the newspaper reader

Professional/executive

Graduated college/post graduate

Age 45+

Household income $50,000+

Married

Own home

Northeast region

Lived at present address 5+ years

Source: MRI, 2004

---

[20]"McSwindle," Kate MacArthur, *Ad Age*, August 27, 2001, p. 1/pp. 22–23.

[21]"Reenergizing Readership and Revitalizing Newspapers," Kubas Consultants. Presented at Newspaper Association of America conference, November 2003.

online for their news). On average, about two thirds (67%) of all newspaper pages are actually opened, a figure that depends in part on the number of pages in the issue. In thinner papers (10–32 pages), 78% of all pages are opened, but when the paper becomes much bigger (81–204 pages), only 63% are opened.

Another consequence of the time readers spend with the paper is that it offers the media specialist more opportunity to provide detailed information. If you are trying to sell a new home equity loan program, then you need the space to provide details on the terms of the deal—as well as on bank locations so interested consumers can find you. Although you might worry that so much fine print will be boring or encourage page-turning, those people who are in your target audience will probably be interested enough to read through the entire ad (assuming the copy is inviting and attention-getting).

Impact of Editorial

An obvious advantage of newspaper advertising is that you can choose the section of the paper in which your ad will appear, for example, putting food ads in the Food Section or offering investment advice in the Business pages. This effectively narrows your reach to those consumers most likely to be interested in your product or service.

Local and Regional Possibilities

Although advertisers are reluctant to use newspapers on a national basis, they rely on them heavily for local or regional marketing. If Procter & Gamble wishes to test a new detergent in Peoria, Illinois, it can advertise in the *Peoria Journal Star* and feel confident that the message will only reach those people able to buy the product, thereby creating awareness for the new item. They might also test the effects of advertising on sales this way. For regional operators, such as Friendly Restaurants (located only in the northeastern part of the country), ads can be placed in newspapers in the selected markets where the restaurant is found.

Even within a market, an advertiser can buy space in only those papers being sold in a certain area. The *Chicago Tribune*, for example, offers eight zoned editions of its daily paper within the Chicago area.

DRAWBACKS OF NEWSPAPER ADVERTISING

As with every medium, newspapers have their own drawbacks as well as benefits. The three most critical drawbacks of newspaper advertisements are short issue life, the challenge of grabbing the reader's attention, and the constraints of using a largely black and white medium.

Today or Never

Whereas magazines can often prolong their issue life and reach more people by being passed around or picked up on several occasions, at the end of each day the newspaper is usually discarded. If the reader misses your ad that day, you are not given a second chance. So, although newspapers are available every day, their issue life is very short.

Active Readers

The issue life of the newspaper is closely linked to how people read it. For although more than one half of all pages are likely to be opened, it is up to the reader to actively choose what to look at. If your headline doesn't attract Jane Doe's attention, then she won't look at it at all; if the copy isn't intriguing and relevant to her, then she can simply turn to another article or page. It is therefore crucial that newspaper advertisements get the reader's attention. When people sit in front of the television or listen to the radio, they are generally a "passive" audience with no choice but to attend to the ad (even if fleetingly) or turn off the radio or TV set. Exhibit 4.15 shows how the newspaper advertiser must fight for attention.

Black and White

In the 1980s, it was rare to find a color ad in a newspaper. Then the Gannett Corporation's national newspaper *USA Today* began to offer full-color capabilities. The quality of newspaper color reproduction has been improving ever since, although it is still a long way from looking as sharp as magazine pages (due primarily to the poorer quality of the paper it is printed on).

EXHIBIT 4.15   Elements That Get Newspaper Reader's Attention

Color
Full Page
Photography and illustrations
Product in use
Sale price

Source: Roper Starch Study conducted on behalf of Newspaper Association of America, 2001.

Even so, newspapers charge a premium for use of color, generally about 17% extra for a one-page four-color ad. For many advertisers, particularly those who wish to show "lifelike" qualities such as food manufacturers, it remains more effective to use magazine or television ads.

Research on Newspapers

Although the newspaper industry, through its trade association, the Newspaper Association of America, conducts annual research on the size and strength of the industry, and periodic studies on the medium's effectiveness, academic research has been more limited in recent years. Some studies have been done on the impact of ad size on consumer responses, including work on different promotional formats for the ads.[22]

MAGAZINES—AN EXPLOSION OF CHOICE

Although magazines have a long history in the United States, with the earliest publications appearing in the middle of the 18th century, they are also a medium that may be said to have had two very distinct life stages. Originally, most magazines catered to a very general audience, offering a mixture of news, stories, and features aimed either at the total population or, in the case of titles such as *Ladies' Home Journal* and *Good Housekeeping*, at women. The strength of publications such as *Life*, *Look*, and the *Saturday Evening Post* is reflected in the fact that an ad placed in those magazines in the 1950s would be likely to reach about 60% of the total population.

But with the rise of television in the 1950s, general interest magazines found they could not compete effectively either for advertising dollars or for readers. Rather than simply disappearing, magazines began to move toward greater specialization in their targeting and their editorial content. This trend continues today, with narrowly focused magazines devoted to

---

[22]"The Advertising Exposure Effect of Free Standing Inserts," Srini S. Srinivasan, Robert P. Leone and Francis J. Mulhern, *Journal of Advertising*, vol. 24, no. 1, Spring 1995, 29–40. "Ad Size as an Indicator of Perceived Advertising Costs and Effort: The Effects on Memory and Perceptions," Pamela M. Homer, *Journal of Advertising*, vol. 24, no. 4, Winter 1995, 1–12. "Predictors of Advertising Avoidance in Print and Broadcast Media," Paul Surgi Speck and Michael T. Elliott, *Journal of Advertising*, vol. 26, no. 2, Summer 1997, 61–76. "Communicating in Print: A Comparison of Consumer Responses to Different Promotional Formats," Kenneth R. Lord and Sanjay Putrevu, *Journal of Current Issues and Research in Advertising*, vol. 20, no. 2, Fall 1998, 1–18. "The Information Content of Newspaper Advertising," Avery M. Abernethy, *Journal of Current Issues and Research in Advertising*, vol. 14, no. 2, Fall 1992, 63–68.

topics such as tropical fish (*Tropical Fish Hobbyist*), cross-stitching (*Simply Cross Stitch!*), or aircraft (*Affordable Aircraft*). And whereas there are still some general offerings, such as *Atlantic Monthly* or the *New Yorker*, their readership is considerably lower than the audience of their general interest forebears. Because of this increased specialization, today there are more than 6,000 different consumer magazines available. In 2004 alone, 480 new titles were introduced.

Magazines Today

Despite this specialization, magazines as a medium reach a broad range of the population. Indeed, 94% of all adults read magazines in any one year, buying about six different titles in that time period. The places they purchase them include supermarkets (accounting for 38% of all magazines sold individually), discount stores, book stores, and drug stores. Readers look at each magazine copy for an average of 45 minutes.

There are three main types of magazines: consumer, farm, and business-to-business. Consumer magazines are usually categorized according to their editorial content, such as business, men's, women's, sports, news, and entertainment. This category includes titles enjoyed by all segments of the population, from *Time* to *Sports Illustrated* to *Cosmopolitan*. Farm magazines are geared toward that particular industry. Some may be crop-specific, such as *Cotton Farming*, and others deal with the technical aspects of agriculture. The third type, business-to-business, covers all titles aimed at the industrial user, everything from *Chemical Age* to *Offshore Drilling* to *Information Week*.

Taken together, magazines account for 5% of all ad dollars spent in the United States. Most magazines are considered as national vehicles for advertising, although city or regional publications are also classified within the consumer segment, such as *Milwaukee* or *Southern Living*. More and more, however, national magazines offer geographic breakouts of their circulation allowing an advertiser to place a message that will, for example, only reach southerners, or people who live in the northeast states, or in the Los Angeles metropolitan area. They are also developing more demographic "splits," so that Fidelity Investments can advertise its mutual funds in the edition of *Business Week* that is read by people earning $75,000 or more per year.

Magazines are sold in one of two ways: at the newsstand or by subscription. For most titles, it is the latter that generates the most sales, accounting on average for 86% of a title's circulation. As with newspapers, magazines are assessed in terms of their circulation. Today's top circulation magazines are shown in Exhibit 4.16.

EXHIBIT 4.16	Top 10 magazines by circulation	

Rank	Title	Circulation
1	AARP The Magazine	22,617,093
2	Reader's Digest	10,081,577
3	TV Guide	9,015,544
4	Better Homes & Gardens	7,626,088
5	National Geographic	5,474,135
6	Good Housekeeping	4,639,941
7	Family Circle	4,267,535
8	Woman's Day	4,209,130
9	Ladies' Home Journal	4,120,087
10	Time	4,034,061

Source: Adweek Hot List, 3/14/05, SR19

BENEFITS OF MAGAZINES TO ADVERTISERS

To an advertiser, three of the most attractive qualities of magazines are their high-end audiences, the enthusiasm of those audiences, and the long issue life of the medium.

Upscale Audiences

One of the incentives to using magazines for your advertising message is the favorable demographic profile of magazine readers. Similar to newspaper readers, the heaviest users of this medium are those adults who are age 18 to 44 years, have a college education and a household income over $75,000, and are employed in a professional or managerial job.

Getting Attention

Another benefit of placing your ads in magazines is reader involvement. This concept is rather difficult to define (and even harder to measure), but it generally refers to the interest that the reader has in the material, both editorial and advertising. Because most magazines today focus on a particular subject or interest, they can tie in more readily with the personal needs and lifestyles of the audience, enabling advertisers to do so as well. In this way, automakers can target car enthusiasts or prospective buyers in *Car and Driver* or *Road and Track*, detergent manufacturers can promote their new or improved products in magazines aimed at homemakers (*Better Homes and Gardens*, *Good Housekeeping*, *Ladies Home Journal*), and financial services companies can offer their mutual funds to interested investors in *Fortune* or *Money*.

Consumers also seem less resistant to seeing ads in magazines. One study conducted for the magazine industry in 2004 found that whereas 62% of those surveyed agreed that the advertising on network TV gets in the way of their enjoyment, for magazines the figure was only 28% of respondents. Moreover, nearly half (48%) said that advertising in fact adds to their enjoyment when reading magazines, a proportion that was higher than for any other medium. These findings are in part due to the fact that as a reader, you get to select what ads you read, whereas with television the ads are more or less forced on you (the remote control notwithstanding). Internet advertising is seen, by most users, as mere "clutter" on the screen.

Readers react to magazine ads in a different way than to ads on television. People tend to retain information seen in magazines longer because they can read up to five times faster than they can take in the spoken word. They tend to trust magazine ads more, placing greater faith in the authority of the printed word. And, in many instances, reading a magazine can be considered a pre-shopping experience, allowing consumers the chance to compare products and services and learn new information about an Apple iPod, for example, prior to purchasing it.

Hanging Around

Another important, and unique, feature of magazines is their *long issue life*. Whereas the television program is over in half an hour, and the newspaper is thrown out after one day, you will probably keep a monthly magazine in your home for 4 weeks or longer. This not only gives you opportunities for additional or repeat exposures to the advertising, it is also likely that other people, known as the *secondary* audience, may see the issue too. The importance of this *passalong* readership is shown by the fact that the average magazine is seen by four different readers, with each one spending about 61 minutes with the issue.

DRAWBACKS OF MAGAZINE ADVERTISING

Magazines also have their drawbacks. Among the most significant obstacles to keep in mind are the considerable lead time necessary and the relatively high cost of reaching your targeted audience.

Long Planning Cycle

For most publications, ads have to be completed and at the printer well in advance of their publishing date, a factor known as the *lead time*. This makes it difficult for advertisers to create particularly timely or newsworthy ads of the kind seen in newspapers. Moreover, despite the generally excellent color reproduction quality, the magazine remains two-dimensional (aside from pop-up displays or inserts, discussed further later). This prevents the magazine ad from offering the truly lifelike qualities of a television spot.

Reaching Readers

The increasingly targeted nature of magazines means that the cost of reaching one thousand members of the audience (the *CPM* explained in greater detail in chapter 5) is higher than that of a broader, mass medium such as television. Even some of a magazine's benefits can be viewed as potential disadvantages for you as a media specialist. The notion of readers' involvement with the magazine also means that if they are not very interested in a particular product or ad they can easily ignore it by turning to the next page.

RESEARCH ON MAGAZINES

Studies on magazines as a medium have focused on similar areas as broadcast research. The value of the context in which an ad is seen was found, by Norris and Colman, to impact consumer recall and recognition of the ad.[23] The same topic was explored further by Yi to see what happened when readers were given additional information prior to seeing the magazine ad in its context.[24] Meanwhile, the magazine industry has itself sponsored several studies showing the impact of magazines on sales.[25]

In 2004, the magazine industry sponsored a study undertaken by Northwestern University to examine the motivations for reading magazines. The top 10 reasons included statements such as "I get value for my time and money," "it does not disappoint me," and "it makes me smarter." Several other studies conducted on behalf of magazines have attempted to show how magazine ads provide a better return on advertisers' investment than do other media.

OUTDOOR BILLBOARDS AND BEYOND—FROM CAIRO, EGYPT, TO CAIRO, ILLINOIS

There are some in the outdoor industry who like to claim that billboards are the oldest medium in existence. They date it back to Egyptian times

---

[23]"Context Effects on Recall and Recognition of Magazine Advertisements," Claire E. Norris and Andrew M. Colman, *Journal of Advertising*, vol, 21, no. 3, September 1992, 37–46.

[24]"Contextual Priming Effects in Print Advertisements: The Moderating Role of Prior Knowledge," Youjae Yi, *Journal of Advertising*, vol. 22, no. 1, March 1993, 1–10.

[25]See Magazine Publishers of America (MPA) Web site at magazine.org for more information on Millward Brown study on ad effectiveness, the AC Nielsen Sales Scan Study, and econometric modeling case analysis, *Measuring the Mix*.

when hieroglyphics were written on roadside stones to give people directions to the nearest town or village. Whether or not you agree with that, outdoor billboards are certainly well established, having been around in this country since the 1800s. At that time, companies began leasing space on boards for bills to be pasted (hence the term *billboard*). The two main types of billboard are poster panels and painted bulletins. Panels come in several sizes, named according to the number of sheets of paper originally needed to cover them, such as 8-sheets and 30-sheets. Posters are found mostly in populated areas, in or near cities and towns. Painted bulletins are larger boards situated along highways and major roads. Their name refers to the fact that they were originally painted by hand at the site.

Putting messages on outdoor boards used to be extremely labor intensive. The sheets for poster panels were pasted onto the board, whereas bulletins were hand-painted. Both were created either at the board site or at a central location within the market or region. Because this had to be done in each market, differences resulted in the look of the message from one market to another (and even one site to another within the market). Today, thanks to computer technology, poster panel messages are created electronically and then shipped either in one piece or in sections to the board site. Bulletins still tend to be hand-painted, but computers are now used to make sure that the finished product looks identical across boards. Today, bulletins are often created using other materials, such as lithography or special stretch vinyl.

In the past 40 years, the industry has come under increased criticism from environmentalists who claim that the boards are a blight on the scenery. Many cities and several states have introduced bans on putting up new boards and, in certain cases, demanded the removal of existing structures. For example, you won't see any billboards in Hawaii or Vermont.

Unlike other media that have editorial material too, outdoor billboards exist solely for advertising messages. They are primarily a local medium, bought on a market-by-market basis, but are used by both national and local advertisers. The type of business using the medium has changed considerably in the past 20 years. For many years, the biggest advertiser was the tobacco industry, but 1999 legislation prohibited the advertising of tobacco messages on any outdoor billboards. This not only had a significant impact on the tobacco industry, it freed up many high-profile and well-positioned billboards across the country for other advertisers who had never been able to buy that space because the tobacco companies had long-term deals with the billboard companies. Today, you are far more likely to see billboards from local retailers, the travel industry, or health care providers than you would have even 5 years ago (see Exhibit 4.17 which shows the top ten outdoor advertising categories).

For many years, outdoor billboard audiences were calculated from manual traffic counts conducted by each system operator of how many cars passed by a given billboard, multiplied by government statistics that are up-

EXHIBIT 4.17   Top outdoor advertising categories

Rank	Category	Dollars in thousands
1	Services & amusements	$449,688.8
2	Media & advertising	$323,217.9
3	Public transportation, hotels & resorts	$292,744.4
4	Retail	$283,351.8
5	Insurance & real estate	$247,762.8
6	Financial	$220,398.3
7	Automotive dealers & services	$210,429.3
8	Restaurants	$204,228.6
9	Automotive, auto accessories & equipment	$183,123.5
10	Communications	$161,654.0

Source: TNS Sofres, 2005

dated periodically on how many people are present in the average car. That became the estimated audience viewing a billboard. In 2001, the outdoor industry's auditing organization, the Traffic Audit Bureau, introduced an automated system to count the traffic. It uses special software that looks at traffic counts by road segments within a market, and uses those to come up with the audience figures. This avoids inconsistent counting done by different operators within and across markets, as well as removing some of the human error involved in that process.

In 2004, outdoor audience measurement took several new strides forward, with the testing by both Arbitron and Nielsen of Global Positioning by Satellite (GPS) devices to help figure out to which boards consumers had been exposed. Both companies tested this approach in selected markets, with the goal of expanding it further if it could be shown to provide a more accurate, yet still affordable, alternative means of capturing ad exposure.

The outdoor industry is far more expansive than it used to be. For example, outdoor messages are now quite commonly seen painted on the sides of buildings, on telephone kiosks and bus shelters, or in sports stadiums. More is said on this in the section, Alternative Forms of Communication.

BENEFITS OF OUTDOOR BILLBOARDS TO ADVERTISERS

The advantages of billboard advertising have contributed to the medium's popularity over the past two centuries. Four of the most consistent and important benefits are size, mobility, effective reach, and cost. Each of these advantages is discussed next.

Big Is Better

The large size of the poster panel or painted bulletin means that outdoor advertising gets noticed. In fact, at a typical busy location in the center of a city, more than 10,000 people are likely to pass an 8-sheet poster panel within a given month. In addition, the message is there constantly for 12 to 24 hours (and many posters are illuminated at night).

Mobility

Not only can painted billboards be moved around an area to expose more of the target to the message, but the outdoor messages can be designed for specific locations, audiences, or activities. So you could place ads for Samsonite luggage aimed at businesspeople at airports to catch them when they travel, or advertise Chiquita bananas near the A&P supermarket where your target audience shops.

Reaching Ethnic Groups

Outdoor billboards allow you to tailor your message to members of a particular ethnic group using their own language or culture yet still reach a mass audience within a specific market. You can buy space in areas with heavy concentrations of Hispanic people, for example, reaching them where they live, work, and shop. It is harder to reach a large portion of these groups with traditionally "Anglo" television or magazines. Furthermore, it is valuable to be able to reach nonnative English speakers in their first language, whatever language that might be.

Reinforcing the Message

Outdoor advertising is a good supplementary medium, helping to add reach and frequency to a media schedule at reasonable cost. A fairly typical outdoor buy could reach over 80% of adults in a given area in a month. In addition, the fact that the billboard is there all the time means that frequency builds up and the message can be a constant reminder. Because many panels are situated in shopping areas, an advertiser can present his message very close to the point of purchase.

DRAWBACKS OF OUTDOOR BILLBOARD ADVERTISING

In considering what part of your advertising budget to commit to outdoor billboard advertising, you will need to keep in mind the two drawbacks of the medium: short exposure time and the potential for criticism from environmentalists.

Brief Message Exposure

The average outdoor message is only seen for between 3 and 7 seconds, so the copy needs to be extremely concise and compelling. For products that need a lot of explanation, outdoor is clearly not the right medium. One way to gauge whether or not there is too much copy on a billboard is to estimate how quickly people are going to pass by it. You can try the exercise yourself, and see how much of the message you can take in as you drive or walk by. Because most of the viewing is done at high speed, especially for bulletins situated along the highway, the advertisement must also be eye-catching and interesting enough to attract the driver's (or passenger's) attention.

Environmental Criticism

The outdoor industry, as noted earlier, has come under increasing criticism for cluttering up the environment. Advertisers might shy away from the medium to avoid legal or ethical disputes, especially in areas with a recent history of environmental controversies.

Research on Outdoor

The outdoor industry is one of the least researched of any mass medium. Studies have focused mostly on proving that the medium works, as shown by Bhargava et al.[26] More information on how the medium has been researched can be found on the Web site of the Outdoor Advertising Association of America (www.oaaa.org).

INTERNET—THE ULTIMATE CHOICE

The rapid growth of the Internet as a consumer medium in the 1990s was unprecedented in the history of media. Internet penetration rose faster than any other medium (or appliance), reaching the critical mass of 50 million users in 5 short years (it took radio 36 years to get to that point). Today, with nearly three quarters (70%) of the country accessing the Internet from home, work, school, or some other location, the medium's capabilities continue to expand and develop. That is due, in part, to the ability of users to access the Web through high-speed (broadband) technology. Today, about half of all users can do so, allowing them easier and faster access to full video offerings.

---

[26]"Improving the Effectiveness of Outdoor Advertising: Lessons From a Study of 282 Campaigns," Mukesh Bhargava, Naveen Donthu, and Rosanne Caron, *Journal of Advertising Research*, vol. 34, no. 2, March/April 1994, 46–55.

The Internet was first devised as a means of communication for the academic community, more than 30 years ago. It was a fairly arcane and complex system, relying on a lot of computer language and processing. The hypertext markup language (HTML) that formed the basis of the Web is now seamlessly (and invisibly) connected to everything we do on the computer. That was not the case originally. It was not until the late 1990s that the Internet came to be seen as a genuine medium (as opposed to computer tool), and one that offered users far greater control than with any other existing medium. Even more so than print media, the Internet lets you select exactly where you want to go and what you want to see. You choose where to click, and how long to stay there. Although you can browse through a magazine or newspaper, you generally have to look at each page (or a table of contents) to find what you are most interested in. On the Web, you can type in a web address (www.mediahandbook.com) and be taken straight to that specific piece of information, without having to wade through other pages in which you have no interest. At the same time, the computer is keeping track of your every movement, capturing each site you visit, and each page within that site. This information proved invaluable in the development of the medium for advertising.

Indeed, as companies began setting up Web sites (a fairly inexpensive proposition), they saw huge potential for advertising to help generate revenues. Analogies to the direct response industry are common. Companies were immediately able to track visits to their sites (by computer address only), and offer advertisers more information on who was not only visiting their sites, but also looking at the ads—and clicking through to the advertiser's site—than any other mass medium. They did so by placing special software, known as *cookies* on users' computers, to monitor the path that users take as they browse different sites on the Internet. Internet ad revenues doubled each year for several years in a row in the late 1990s, surpassing total ad revenues for the outdoor and syndicated TV industries, and by 2004 had reached $6.8 billion.

At first, Internet ads consisted of banners—billboards on the Web—that did little more than offer a brand name or teaser, and a link to another site. Companies began to consider using web advertising for brand-building purposes, rather than simply to offer information. And before long, the ability to purchase via the Web became mainstream rather than exceptional. Today, according to e-Marketer, 74% of the online population age 13+ has made a purchase over the Web. Before long, advertisers started to get more creative, changing the size of the ad message, and incorporating (as technology advanced) more sound, motion, and visual stimulation (e.g., animation), a phenomenon known as *rich media*. Not surprisingly, the research findings showed that these kinds of ads had greater impact (recall, awareness) than the plain-vanilla banners. But it became more clear that as fast as advertisers moved to surprise consumers, those consumers became increasingly disenchanted with web ads.

Today, when most consumers are asked about web advertising, their response is primarily one of irritation. They talk about the "clutter" of Web sites, the irrelevance of most ads that appear, and their techniques for avoiding them. In particular, annoyance with ads that pop up, or pop under, a Web site is considerable. At the same time, if an ad appears on the Web that is relevant and informative, consumers will click on it to find out more. For many, the line between the "editorial" material and the "advertising" is a narrow one on the Web, which is viewed by most people as an information cornucopia.

Another Internet phenomenon that has had an increasing impact on how advertisers think about and use the Web has been the growth of search advertising. Inspired by sites like Google, which allow users to type in any word and find out what is available throughout the Web, advertisers started to realize that they could "buy" keywords or links, and deliver ad messages to consumers when they requested those words. So, for example, if you do a search on Google for the words "razor blades" to find out if your product with a built-in counter is available, at the top of the screen you might see sponsored links from Web sites such as drugstore.com or manufacturers like Gillette or Braun.

Today, search has become the most popular way for advertisers to reach online consumers. They now spend more on search than on "regular" display online ads; indeed, 4 in every 10 online ad dollars go toward search.

BENEFITS OF INTERNET TO ADVERTISERS

In many ways, the benefits of this emerging medium for advertisers are still being explored. Four of the current advantages are flexibility, personalization, reach, and measurability.

Flexibility

There are many forms of Internet advertising. Unlike other mass media, where choices come down to 15- or 30-second commercials or full page versus half-page ads, the Internet does not limit the imagination. From traditional banner ads to pop ups to search, ad messages can appear in numerous forms. Beyond that, advertisers are increasingly trying to communicate with prospects via e-mail, asking people to *opt-in* and be willing to receive messages that way, offering them cut-price travel deals on Travelocity, or the best-seller list on Amazon. Advertisers can also engage in affiliate marketing, where one site promotes another site's products or services in exchange for some commission on the sale.

Targeted Message

The Internet is the first mass medium able to offer a targeted, personal advertising message. Although direct response has been doing so for many years, it was not possible in TV, radio, newspapers, magazines, or billboards to talk to anything less than a sizable audience. With the Internet, however, advertisers are actually able to send messages to named individuals (via opt-in e-mail marketing). It is assumed that such messages, by being more relevant to that individual, are more likely to be accepted and absorbed.

Reach

Although the Internet does not offer as broad a reach as television, campaigns that appear on a range of Web sites (particularly the gateway or portal sites many people have as their home pages, (e.g., msn.com or yahoo.com) can indeed reach a high proportion of everyone on the Internet. In addition, the reach on the Internet can be given against specific advertising messages, not just the sites on which those messages appear (i.e., ad exposure not just opportunity to see).

Measurability

For advertisers, the Internet's ability to measure who is doing what on the Web would seem to be answering one of the "holy grail" questions of the industry. But because the measurement is computer-based rather than person-based, the measures are in fact not as precise and valuable as they might appear. Having said that, Internet measurement is certainly far more detailed than for any other mass medium, where at best the media specialist can look at opportunities to be exposed to the ad, rather than actual viewer, reader, or listener behavior. Several advertisers have undertaken cross-media studies of ad impact on the Web compared to other media (using statistical modeling) and found that the Internet ads are usually more effective at enhancing brand image and consideration than other media types.[27] Initially, web advertising was sold based on *click throughs* (users clicking on web ad to link to advertisers' sites), but it soon became clear that if Internet advertising was to be comparable to other ad media, then the cost metric had to be the same. Today, most sites price their advertising based on cost per thousand (CPM). Web measurement services provide data on the demographics and lifestyles of web users, as well as web traffic to individual sites and/or ads.

---

[27]"How the Internet is Reshaping Advertising," Rex Briggs, *Admap*, Issue 560, April 2005, 59–61.

DRAWBACKS OF INTERNET ADVERTISING

As new and exciting as the Internet is, it still cannot provide advertisers with everything they would want to reach their desired targets. Here is a summary of the downside to Internet advertising, in terms of consumer irritation, confusion, and nonstandard metrics.

Consumer Irritation

The plethora of advertising on the Internet is not always appreciated by consumers. Although users have the option to click on an ad to find out more information, there are more messages that pop up or "pop under" a site that users have to actively remove if they do not want to look at them. Moreover, because people tend to use the Web to look for specific information (rather than passively consuming a TV program or browsing a magazine's pages), the irritation level with the high number of ad messages on a web page (banners, buttons, sponsorships) can become overwhelming, detracting from the impact of any one particular message.

Confusion

Although this particular drawback reflects, to a large extent, the newness of the medium, many Internet users remain fairly unsophisticated in how they use the Web, uncertain of what will happen if they click on an ad, for example ("Will I get back to the page that I really wanted to be on?"). There is also a more generalized confusion among many users about what in fact constitutes a web advertisement. Is it a company's Web site (e.g., nike.com)? Or, are the pages that pop up in moving from one page to another (so-called *interstitials*) ad messages or actual sites? Although some of this confusion may benefit advertisers (putting out messages that users see as information rather than advertising), the confusion is as likely to lead to avoidance as interaction.

Nonstandard Metrics

As a relatively new ad medium, the Internet has not yet developed fully standardized measurement metrics. Each measurement service uses slightly different methods (not always fully revealed) to measure a different list of Web sites. Some sites try to sell advertising based on audience impressions, others on site visits (clicks), and yet others on actual sales. As the medium matures, it is likely that more standardization will be put in place, especially to make it more comparable to traditional mass media.

RESEARCH ON THE INTERNET

A study conducted on behalf of the Online Publishers Association (OPA) in 2005 found that when Internet users were more engaged in the content, they not only spent more time with a site, but also were more likely to recommend it to their friends. Through both qualitative and quantitative studies, and segmentation of the data, the OPA uncovered 22 distinct online user experiences, ranging from "connection with others" to "worth saving and sharing." The experiences most likely to increase online usage included content that was entertaining and absorbing, and content that was personalized ("looks out for people like me").[28]

Others have started to try to model the uses and gratifications of Internet use, finding that those looking for information tend to interact more with messages on Web sites, whereas those looking for social interaction turn to the Web for human-to-human communication.[29]

There is an abundance of additional research on the Internet.[30]

ALTERNATIVE FORMS OF COMMUNICATION

As the traditional media forms already outlined grow increasingly cluttered, advertisers are looking for new and different ways to present their messages to the target audience. Some of the most important means available are Yellow Pages, in-store advertising, sponsorship, and word of mouth.

Yellow Pages

Although placed under nontraditional media, Yellow Pages advertising has been in existence for almost as long as the telephone directory itself. Offering advertisers (and consumers) another type of classified advertising, the Yellow Pages generated $14 billion in advertising revenues in 2004. There are nearly 7,000 different Yellow Pages directories in the United States, distinguished not just by location (Chicago vs. New York) but also by target (the "silver" pages targeting senior citizens or the gay/lesbian directory for that consumer group). This can sometimes make it harder for advertisers because of the lack of standardization in terms of ad sizes or guidelines.

---

[28]"Online User Experience Study," Online Publishers Association, 2005.

[29]"Internet Uses and Gratifications," Hanjun Ko, Chang-Hoan Cho, and Marilyn S. Roberts, *Journal of Advertising*, vol. 34, no. 2, Summer 2005, 57–70.

[30]See, e.g., "Displacement and Reinforcement Effects of the Internet and Other Media as Sources of Information," Stanley D. Sibley and James C. Tsao, *Journal of Advertising Research*, vol. 44, no. 1, March 2004, 126–142. "Changing Fortunes for Internet Advertising," Chris Dobson, *Admap*, Issue 448, March 2004, 32–33. "Determinants of Internet Advertising: An Empirical Study," George Baltas, *International Journal of Market Research*, vol. 45, no. 4, 505–513. "Banner Advertiser-Web Site Context Congruity and Color Effects on Attention and Attitudes," Robert S. Moore, Claire Allison Stammerjohan, and Robin A. Coulter, *Journal of Advertising*, vol. 34, no. 2, Summer 2005, 71–84.

People use the Yellow Pages to look up information and services. More than one fifth of the time, the search is related to business needs. The top three categories that people turn to are food, dining out and entertainment, and automotive. The top three headings in Yellow Pages directories in terms of the number of listings are restaurants, physicians and surgeons, and auto parts.

According to Mediamark Research, Inc. (MRI), about one quarter of the population has used the Yellow Pages in the past 7 days, and nearly two thirds (63%) have done so within the past 12 months. But 60% of the 3% of the country who moved in the past year used the Yellow Pages, as did 19% of the 99% of the country who ordered a pizza. The "average" profile is someone who is between age 25 and 49, has been to college, and has an annual household income of $60,000 or more.

Within the past few years, there have been some new developments in Yellow Pages advertising. First, the industry has attempted to attract more national advertisers, who accounted for just 15% of total revenues in 2004. For most consumers, the Yellow Pages are usually considered a means of finding local information. In 2004, the Association of National Advertisers (ANA) hired one company to provide measurement for a new syndicated yellow pages service that uses telephone surveys to estimate usage of the medium and recall overall and in key product categories.[31]

Today, there are other places to go for Yellow Pages information. Most prominent among these is the Internet, where sites like switchboard.com or 411.com let people search for what or who they want online. For most people, however, the Internet and printed copies of the Yellow Pages are not mutually exclusive. One survey found that 80% of the people who had shopped online in an average month had also looked at the printed version in that same timeframe.

The availability of color in the Yellow Pages has helped some advertisers gain additional attention from consumers. In a study conducted by Fernandez and Rosen, ads were seen as more informative and noticeable when color was included.[32] Research by Laband and Abernathy looked at the impact of different sized Yellow Pages ads, and as expected, larger size ads generate more response, although not in an exponential fashion, whereas the number of competitive advertisers under the same heading has a negative impact on response.[33]

---

[31]"Putting a 21st-Century Spin on a Powerful Selling Vehicle," Burt Michaels, *Know Magazine*, 51–58.

[32]"The Effectiveness of Information and Color in Yellow Pages Advertising," Karen V. Fernandez and Dennis L. Rosen, *Journal of Advertising*, vol. 29, no. 2, Summer 2000, 59–72.

[33]"The Customer Pulling Power of Different-Sized Yellow Pages Advertising," Avery M. Abernathy and David N. Laband, *Journal of Advertising Research*, vol. 42, no. 3, May/June 2002, 66–72.

In-Store Advertising

Just like Yellow Pages advertising, the notion of placing advertising messages inside stores is not especially new. Signs and promotions have been available in stores for more than 25 years. Today, however, more advertisers are including in-store media explicitly in the media plan, acknowledging this as advertising rather than simply a promotional expense. In 2004, advertisers spent an astonishing $18.5 billion in this venue. One of the main reasons for its increased popularity is that it is the most measurable of all media. Thanks to electronic scanning at the cash register, advertisers are able to see what happens at the checkout counter when their messages are in the store. Some of the most popular locations for in-store messages are on the shelf displays, on TV screens at the checkout, or "floor signs" next to the freezer cabinet or in the aisles. In addition, messages or coupons can be generated at the checkout counter when people pay for their goods, tailored to the purchases that have just been made. This form of advertising has moved from grocery stores to a wide variety of retail outlets, including Wal-Mart and Circuit City.

In-store advertising effectively eliminates the time between seeing the message and buying the item. Drawbacks include the possibility that the target misses the ad somehow, either by not paying attention or by its being covered up in some way. In addition, in-store advertising is not especially cheap. It tends to have its greatest effect among current brand users rather than persuading buyers of the competitor's brand to switch. The time for message exposure is very short, so messages tend to focus on price and be extremely brief.

Sponsorship

As advertisers have had to work harder to reach their target consumers, one of the nontraditional forms of communication they have turned to is sponsorship. This involves paying an organization a fee to put a company or brand name at the head of an event or as the key sponsor of that event. Examples include State Farm Insurance's sponsorship of an ice skating competition, to Visa's sponsorship of the U.S. Olympic team, to the renaming of sports stadiums after companies (e.g., American Airlines Center in Dallas, Philips Arena in Atlanta, and SBC Center in San Antonio). The practice of sponsorship is now estimated to be worth $9.5 billion.

The majority of sponsorship spending (69%) goes toward sports-related events, followed by entertainment tours and attractions (9%), and festivals, fairs, and annual events (8%). A rapidly growing area within the sponsorship area is cause-related marketing, where companies link up with non-profit groups and become "sponsors" of their causes. Examples include Avon's support of an annual 3-day walk to raise funds for breast cancer research, and Tanqueray's sponsorship of a bike ride each summer to raise money for AIDS. Even though sponsorship is generally considered to be undertaken to reach a national audience, there are often significant local opportunities too. Sponsorship of local sports teams can enhance a company's reputation in those particular markets; and companies that choose to sponsor a local annual festival often receive positive coverage in the local media. There are also benefits to be gained by sponsoring grassroots or community festivals and fairs, especially among ethnic audiences.

The reasons companies choose sponsorship instead of (or more likely in addition to) traditional advertising are many. They include the opportunity for heightened visibility for their brand name, thereby increasing the chances of shaping positive consumer attitudes ("I like ice skating, therefore since State Farm sponsors a skating competition, I like State Farm more too"). Sometimes, sponsorship works well for smaller companies. Although they may have smaller ad budgets compared to bigger competitors, their sponsorship of a key event or attraction can make them seem an equal in consumers' eyes. Coors Brewing Company spends far less on advertising than either Anheuser-Busch or Miller Beers, but when all three companies are sponsoring race cars at NASCAR events, the viewer or attendee does not see one company as a better or necessarily bigger sponsor than another. One of the potential downsides of sponsorship was seen in 2002 when the giant energy trading company, Enron, found itself bankrupt and subject to numerous criminal investigations for its financial practices. The company's earlier purchase of the naming rights for Houston's arena, which they called Enron Field, no longer seems as smart a decision as before.

The media are getting more actively involved in creating sponsorships for advertisers. *Cooking Light* magazine created a "healthy" house filled with products of its sponsoring companies, such as Reebok (exercise equipment), Lennox Industries (air conditioning), and Whirlpool (appliances). The magazine promoted the house in its pages and attracted thousands of visitors to its Birmingham, Alabama, location. After the promotion ended, the magazine was able to sell the home privately. Sponsorships are not only aimed at adults these days. Mattel, the company that makes Barbie dolls, took part in a shopping mall tour with *Better Homes & Gardens* magazine, sponsoring a girl's bedroom showcasing Barbie-themed products such as furniture and bedding.

Word of Mouth

Although considered by many to not be a true "medium," per se, word of mouth is becoming an increasingly popular way for advertisers to promote their brands. It is sometimes referred to as "viral" marketing, using the metaphor of spreading good words about a brand the way that a virus can spread among people. In particular, products that are new or are targeting specific groups may lend themselves to this form of promotion. At its simplest, word of mouth involves getting the (positive) word out to people who are considered opinion leaders in a particular category, so that they will then influence others to consider the brand. Some marketers take it further, and plant people in key venues where the brand is either used (e.g., a new vodka in a bar), and have them talk to the people around them about the wonders of this product. Those consumers are unaware that the individual has been paid to promote the brand, so critics have complained that this is a deceptive, or even unethical, practice.

The use of word of mouth marketing has also spread to cell phones. The goal of viral mobile messages is to have the message spread from person to person as they pass it along to their family and friends. Some ringtones have become popular this way, particularly among teens and young adults. However, there is the danger that these messages will be considered "junk" or "spam," and ignored or discarded.

WHICH MEDIA SHOULD YOU USE?

Now that you have some basic information on each major media category, we can start to consider why you might or might not wish to include them in your media plans. To make this process less cumbersome, we'll need to recap some of the most important advantages and disadvantages that each medium offers. These are summarized in Exhibit 4.18.

SUMMARY

Before deciding which media might best be suited to achieving your plan objectives, it is important to consider the advantages and disadvantages that each type of media can offer. Issues to be included in your analysis include the reach and/or frequency of the medium, length of message exposure, audience involvement, clutter, targetability, and cost. For each media category, an examination of the benefits and drawbacks will help determine whether, and to what extent, it should be included in the final plan. Nontraditional alternatives should be considered too, along with the mass media forms.

CHECKLIST—EXPLORING THE MAJOR MEDIA

1. Do you want primarily national or local media in your plan, or a combination of both?

EXHIBIT 4.18 Pros and cons of major media

	Pros	Cons
TV	True to life; pervasive; high reach	Expensive; brief message; clutter; ad positioning
Radio	Local appeal; targeted reach; imagery transfer; low cost; high frequency; flexibility	Background; short message life; fragmentation
Newspaper	Timeliness; desirable audience; editorial impact; local/regional benefits	Short issue life; attention span; black and white
Magazine	Upscale audience; selective exposure; long issue life	Long lead time; high targeted cost
Outdoor	Large size; mobility; low cost; ethnic reach; complement to other media	Brief exposure; environmental issue
Internet	Flexibility; reach; personalization; measurability	Consumer irritation; confusion; non-standard metrics

Other Media

Yellow Pages

In-Store/Marketing At-Retail

Sponsorship

Word of Mouth

2. Will the benefits of television (mass reach, closeness to reality, and pervasiveness) help achieve your media objectives?

3. Have you considered the drawbacks of television (cost, brief exposure time, advertising clutter, and uncertain pod positioning)?

4. Should you use traditional TV ads or explore some of the new forms of TV advertising, such as on DVRs, PPV, or brand integration?

5. Will the benefits of radio (local appeal, targeted formats, low cost, high frequency, and message flexibility) help achieve your media objectives?

6. Have you considered the drawbacks of radio (its background nature, audio-only message, brief exposure time, and fragmented market)?

7. Will the benefits of newspapers (timeliness, editorial affinity, local and regional capabilities, and upscale audiences) help achieve your media objectives?

8. Have you considered the drawbacks of newspapers, such as brief exposure, poor color capabilities, and selective readers?

9. Will the benefits of magazines (upscale audiences, involved and interested readers, and long issue life) help achieve your media objectives?

10. Have you considered the drawbacks of magazines (long lead time, two-dimensional message, and higher costs per thousand)?
11. Will the benefits of outdoor billboards (large message size, rotating message, ethnic targetability) help achieve your media objectives?
12. Have you considered the drawbacks of outdoor billboards (brief message exposure and environmental impact)?
13. Will the benefits of the Internet (flexibility, targeted message, reach, measurability) help achieve your media objectives?
14. Have you considered the drawbacks of the Internet (irritation, confusion, and nonstandard metrics)?
15. Are there opportunities to use Yellow Pages, in-store advertising, sponsorship, or word of mouth in your media plan, to increase the impact of and audience for your message?

Terms, Calculations, and Considerations

Just as computer programmers talk about bits, bytes, and RAM, and car enthusiasts dwell on RPM, jerk, and lateral acceleration, so do media specialists converse in their own language. Before moving on to the actual media plan development, it is helpful to review some of these definitions.

UNDERSTANDING RATINGS

Most of you are probably already familiar with the weekly release of the Nielsen ratings, which identify the most popular television programs. The size of the audience is usually given in absolute terms (i.e., millions of people) and as a percentage of the population. It is this latter figure, known as the *rating,* that is used as the baseline measure for all media concepts.

Rating Point

One rating point equals 1% of a particular target group. That audience can be defined in various ways—by household, by geographic market, or by a given demographic group (e.g., men from 18 to 49 or women from 25 to 54), or by product usage or ownership (e.g., people who own a digital camera). The television program "Survivor" might receive a household rating of 15.3 in Memphis, which means that 15.3% of homes in that city watched the show. The magazine *Entertainment Weekly* might get a rating of 10.2 among females from age 18 to 34, meaning that 10.2% of all women in that age group read that particular issue of the magazine.

Gross Rating Points

By adding up all the rating points we wish to achieve, we end up with a concept known as gross rating points (GRPs). For media planning purposes, we set as our goal a given number of total, or "gross," rating points to achieve and then figure out which vehicles to use to obtain that number. We might want our plan to have a total of 100 gross rating points each week against our target of working women. These could come from any media.

The reason these rating points are considered "gross" is that they do not take into account any duplication of exposure. That is, there are probably many people within our target who see an ad for Slim Fast in *Fitness* and also hear the same message on the local morning talk show. So although our total number of rating points placed in the media each week is set at 100, each person will be exposed to a different number of them and in different vehicles. This is shown in the diagram below.

In today's complex media world, where our targets are becoming more narrowly defined, the term *GRP* is often altered to *TRP*, or "target rating point." This makes explicit the fact that we are planning our ratings against a specific *target,* rather than the whole world. The concept is the same, however.

Gross Impressions

This term simply converts the gross rating points into a number by dividing the number of rating points by 100 and multiplying that figure by the size of

EXHIBIT 5.1   Diagram of GRPs and Duplication

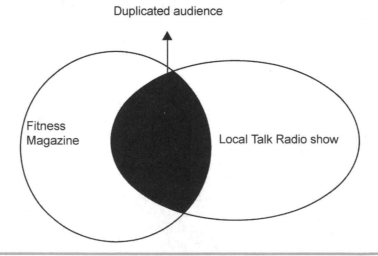

the target audience. So if our plan calls for obtaining 200 GRPs against a target audience of 500,000 people, then we are aiming to achieve 1 million gross impressions (200/100 × 500,000).

REACH AND FREQUENCY

Although many would argue that advertising is more art than science, we still need some way to assess whether or not the messages we place in the media are having any impact. It is not enough to know how many impressions are made with one ad, or what percentage of the target audience is exposed to a given program or magazine. As media specialists, we also need an estimate of the cumulative effect of our media plan. That is provided by the concepts of reach and frequency.

Reach

Reach refers to the number or percentage of people in the target audience who will be exposed to the medium where the message appears. You should note that we can only estimate exposure to the *media vehicle,* not to the ad itself. If you think about your own media habits, then there are many intervening variables that easily prevent you from seeing or hearing an ad. You might deliberately ignore it, turning the page of the magazine or changing the TV channel or avoiding the Web pop-up when it appears. You could be doing something else at the same time, such as talking to a friend or cooking dinner, therefore not paying attention to the message. Or you could find the ad boring, irrelevant, or uninteresting, and see or hear it but not really absorb the contents. So when we talk about the reach of a plan, we are really talking about the opportunity-for-exposure (sometimes called opportunity-to-see, or OTS).

And, of course, we should also emphasize that reach, like all media terms, is merely an estimate. We will never know exactly how many people were reached or how they reacted. But, if we are trying to reach women from age 25 to 54 to persuade them to try our new brand of body wash, then by using syndicated data sources we can find out how many women of that age watch "The View" or read *Redbook*. To reach a target audience of men from age 18 to 49 to increase the number of inquiries for Fidelity Investment's pamphlet on investing wisely, we can learn how many men of that age read a daily newspaper or watch CNN.

The difference between reach and GRPs is that reach concerns the number of *different* people in the audience you are trying to communicate with through advertising. For media schedules that try to maximize reach, you would place ads in several different media vehicles to reach different people through each one. Complicated formulas are used to calculate the numbers, requiring the speed and power of computers. Here, we look at a simple example.

If the rating for *People* against our target of 18- to 49-year-olds is 20 and for *Time* magazine it is 10, then one ad placed in each magazine will deliver a total of 30 GRPs (20 + 10). However, if we know from research that 6% of the target audience will see both ads (the duplicated audience) then the reach, or *unduplicated*, audience for this schedule is 30 – 6, or 24%. That is, 24% of our target of adults from age 18 to 49 will be exposed to our ad in *People and/or* our ad in *Time*. Even if they see both ads they will only be counted in our audience one time. Exhibit 5.2 depicts this situation. So reach = GRPs – duplication.

Frequency

It is not enough to know who our media plan is intended to reach. We must also set goals of *how many times* we wish to reach them with our message. As with the concept of reach, the notion of frequency, although it ultimately refers to *message* frequency, in reality is based on the frequency of exposure to the *media vehicle* rather than to the advertisement. A media plan will typically establish the desired number of times that the audience should be exposed to the message, based on past experience, judgment, or previous research into how long it takes for the audience to comprehend and remember the message.

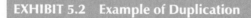

EXHIBIT 5.2   Example of Duplication

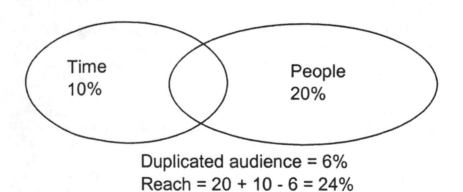

Time
10%

People
20%

Duplicated audience = 6%
Reach = 20 + 10 - 6 = 24%

A simple way to back in to the frequency number is from the following equation:

$$\text{Reach} \times \text{Frequency} = \text{Gross Rating Points}$$

So if you know your reach goal, and you have established the number of GRPs you will be buying, then it only requires simple mathematical division (GRPs/Reach) to figure out how many times, on average, the target will be exposed to the media vehicle(s).

BEYOND REACH AND FREQUENCY

If you think about the commercials that you can remember, what most likely comes to mind are those that you have seen or heard more than once. That is, for a message to be truly *effective* in terms of communicating with the target audience, it generally has to be conveyed more than one time. Now, of course, this is not a hard-and-fast rule. If your bathroom drain gets blocked up, then you only need one exposure to an ad for Drano drain cleaner at the right moment in time, and that message will be extremely effective. But, for the most part, given the limited attention we pay to commercial messages, we need to see or hear them several times before the information is properly absorbed. And, even then, it is most likely filed away somewhere in memory for use on a future occasion.

Effective Frequency

The key here is to determine *how many times* an ad has to be received for it to be deemed effective. What we mean by effective is that the target receives the desired communication message. A considerable amount of research was done on this topic during the 1970s and 1980s, following a landmark study by Colin MacDonald, a British researcher. After looking at the relationship between opportunities to see ads for laundry detergent and sales of the product, he concluded that the optimal number of exposure opportunities was three. This was later explained by breaking down what happens with each exposure. The first time someone sees an ad, his reaction is "what is it?" On the second exposure, he asks "what of it?" or "so what?" It is only on the third occasion that the person will start to process the information and decide whether or not the message is relevant and interesting.[1]

Since those research studies were first published, there has been much controversy over their accuracy. Many have argued that it is impossible to set an ar-

---

[1]"Memory Without Recall, Exposure Without Perception," Herbert E. Krugman, *Journal of Advertising Research*, vol. 40, no. 6, November/December 2000, 49–54.

bitrary number for effective frequency. Some believe that rather than having a single figure, the most effective frequency lies within a range, typically set between 3 and 10. And others claim that only one exposure is needed, as long as it is placed at the right time. This is discussed further in chapter 6. The answer, probably, is "it depends." As with the aforementioned drain cleaner example, sometimes a single exposure is sufficient. On the other hand, you might need to see an ad for a breakfast cereal 15 times before it has any real impact. What it ultimately depends on is the relevancy and impact of the message.[2]

The key point to remember here is that when establishing your media objectives and deciding on the strategy to fulfill them, you must keep in mind that your message should probably be heard, read, or viewed several times in order for it to have an effect on the audience.

Exposure Distribution

Most media plans involve placing multiple ads in many different media vehicles so it is important to know how many people are reached how many times (once, twice, three times, etc.). We find this by creating an *exposure distribution*, which shows the percentage of the target exposed to a given schedule at each level of frequency. The method used to calculate it is fairly complex, based on mathematical theories of probability, and today it is generally done by computer. At a basic level, a media model estimates the likelihood of being exposed to a given number of ads together with the number of different ways you can be exposed to those messages.

For example, if you placed one ad in *Time* and one in *People,* the reader might see anywhere from zero to two ads total—they might not see either ad, or they could see one of the two, or they might see both. Looking at Exhibit 5.2, we already know the percentage of the target exposed two times (the duplication figure) is 6%. In addition, we can easily figure out those not exposed at all (the total, or 100%, minus those exposed one or more times)—100 – 24 = 76%. So to estimate what percentage is reached exactly once you subtract the duplication figure from the number reached one or more times (*reach 1+*)—24 – 6 = 18. You should notice that the final exposure distribution must account for everyone in the target audience and therefore sum to 100%. The final exposure distribution is shown in Exhibit 5.3.

---

[2]"Effective Frequency—Then and Now," Michael J. Naples, *Journal of Advertising Research,* vol. 37, no. 4, July/August 1997, 7–13. "If Not Effective Frequency, Then What?" Kenneth A. Longman, *Journal of Advertising Research,* vol. 37, no. 4, July/August 1997, 44–50. "What Can One Exposure Do?" Lawrence D. Gibson, *Journal of Advertising Research,* vol. 36, no. 1, March/April 1996, 9–18. "Effective Frequency: One Exposure or Three Factors," Gerard Tellis, *Journal of Advertising Research,* vol. 37, no. 4, July/August 1997, 75–80. "Effective Reach and Frequency: Does It Really Make Sense?" Hugh M. Cannon and Edward A. Riordan, *Journal of Advertising Research,* vol. 34, no. 2, March/April 1994, 19–28.

EXHIBIT 5.3 Exposure distribution	
Frequency (f)	Percent reached (%)
0	76
1	18
2	6
Total	100

Frequency Planning

In the late 1990s, research evidence became available suggesting that reach was a more important determinant of media effectiveness than frequency. Based largely on the work of John Philip Jones and Erwin Ephron, the analysis of sales and TV viewing data from the same households suggested that short-term advertising sales were driven largely by exposure to a TV commercial within 7 days prior to purchase. Because we as media specialists never know precisely when that sale might occur, this suggests that it is more important to maintain a lower level of media weight across more weeks than to place sporadic, albeit larger, flights of advertising throughout the year.[3] We revisit this in Chapter 6.[4]

CALCULATING COSTS

It is highly unlikely that you will have *carte blanche* to spend however much money you want or need. You will have to provide some kind of financial explanation of how efficiently your plan will spend your client's money. And because there are many different media types and vehicles that could, potentially, be included in the plan, it is up to the media specialist to rationalize and explain the financial reasoning behind selections.

Cost per Thousand (CPM)

Different media are bought in different ways (a 30-second spot on radio or TV, or a one-page ad in a magazine, or a 30-sheet poster for a billboard), so

---

[3]*The Ultimate Secrets of Advertising*, by John Philip Jones, Sage Publications, 2002; *When Ads Work*, by John Philip Jones, Lexington Books, 1995.

[4]"Recency Planning," Erwin Ephron, *Journal of Advertising Research*, vol. 37, no. 4, July/August 1997, 61–65. "Single Source Research Begins to Fulfill Its Promise," John Philip Jones, *Journal of Advertising Research*, vol. 35, no. 3, May/June 1995, 9–17. "More Weeks, Less Weight: The Shelf Space Model of Advertising," Erwin Ephron, *Journal of Advertising Research*, vol. 35, no. 3, May/June 1995, 18–24.

we need some way to compare media in terms of cost. To do so, media spe-cialists turn to the cost per thousand (CPM). This shows the cost of reaching 1,000 of the target audience either with an individual media vehicle or the complete media schedule. It puts all media on a level playing field and is calculated as follows:

$$\text{CPM} = \text{Total Schedule Cost/Gross Impressions (000)}$$

Let's use an example of 132 million adults from age 18 to 49 and assume that an ad in *Time* costs $235,000, whereas one in *People* costs $215,000. A total of 39 million impressions would be generated (300 TRPs/100 × 132 million adults). At a total cost of $450,000, the cost per thousand would be $11.36. This means it costs $11.36 to reach 1,000 adults from age 18 to 49 with one ad in *Time* and one in *People* in a given month. By using this for-mula, you can compare the cost efficiency of one vehicle, media category, or schedule against another.

Cost per Point (CPP)

Another useful media tool is the cost per rating point (CPP), which offers a different way of comparing media schedules. Here, you find the cost of one rating point for each media vehicle against your target by dividing the total schedule cost by gross rating points:

$$\text{CPP} = \text{Total Schedule Cost/Gross Rating Points}$$

With our total cost of $450,000 and total rating points of 30, the cost per point comes out to be $15,000. It therefore costs $15,000 to obtain one rat-ing point against adults from age 18 to 49 using one ad in *Time* and one in *People*. If you know the cost per point against a particular target group and the approximate number of rating points you wish to buy, then you can then calculate an approximate total schedule cost, using the same formula.

CATEGORY-SPECIFIC CRITERIA

In addition to knowing the general terms that are used in media planning, it is helpful to be familiar with some of the other criteria that are used in se-lecting each major media category. The rest of this chapter outlines these considerations.

Considerations for Television Advertising

The chief currency for a television plan is the program rating. As we do not measure audience exposure to the actual *commercial*, we have to rely on the surrogate number of how many people watched the *program* in which it ran. That data is available from Nielsen Media Research, for both national and local markets. Ratings are collected on a minute-by-minute basis, but until recently, were reported for programs based on the audience size at the mid-minute of the quarter hour. Outside of the United States, viewing data is usually collected every second and reported for each minute. The U.S. viewing data will likely be gathered at this level of detail too, because the digital set-top boxes are capturing that anyway. At the end of 2005, Nielsen Media Research, the company that provides the industry with TV ratings, began releasing actual minute-by-minute data to its clients.

The U.S. TV marketplace operates based on the laws of supply and demand. The more people who watch a particular show, the more expensive it is to advertise within it. The ranges are enormous. You might pay $500,000 or more for a 30-second commercial on network television during prime time, but only a few hundred dollars to have your ad appear on your local TV station during the night. That cost will correspond to the number of people exposed to your ad—millions, versus a few hundred.

In addition to the costs and ratings, it can be helpful to look at the viewers per viewing (or tuning) household, or VPVH numbers (sometimes called VPTH). This figure provides you with an assessment of the concentration of a given demographic group in a program's audience, showing how many people in every thousand viewers fall into that particular category. If the VPVH among women from age 25 to 54 for "All My Children" is 535, and for the "Masters Golf Championship" it is 155, that indicates you will reach more than three times as many women from age 25 to 54 with an ad placed in the soap opera than you will with the golf tournament.

What you should be most interested in, as a media specialist, is finding which programs are going to best reach your target audience. As we noted in chapter 3, although you may have a fairly detailed description of your customer, when it comes to getting data on TV audiences you will end up looking primarily at age and gender. Those are very powerful determinants of product purchase and behavior, so for many goods and services those numbers will suffice. Until the industry finds an affordable and reliable way of measuring TV viewing according to product usage patterns, it is likely that program ratings among broad demographic groups will remain the norm.

One other way to analyze TV viewing behavior in a more in-depth manner is by combining the TV ratings data with lifestyle and other media use information from another source. This process, known as *data fusion*, has been successfully used in many countries. It has been discussed extensively in the research community for many years, and used in the marketplace in many European countries, but only now, in the first decade of the 21st century, are advertisers starting to explore it here in the U.S. What the process involves is "matching" respondents from two different databases, linking them on a number of common variables (gender, age, geographic location, ethnicity, etc.), and then "fusing" the data so that the information unique to one dataset can be used to describe or explain the behavior of all the respondents. It is a complex and intricate process, however, requiring statistical expertise and understanding.

In selecting your TV programs, keep in mind that the list may be changed when the commercial time is bought. The plan is just that—a *plan* of which media vehicles are desired. When negotiations take place, it may be that other programs are included, or some of your recommendations rejected, based on other considerations such as cost and availability. What you should emphasize, however, is the *daypart* that you wish your ads to appear in, because although people do tend to watch individual programs rather than time periods, there is more similarity in the kinds of programs watched within time periods than across them. Alternatively, you may wish to specify the *program type*, or genre so that the buy focuses on comedies, for example, or news programming, regardless of when it airs.

The criteria you use to evaluate which programs to use for television do not vary whether you are planning to use network, spot, syndication, or cable. If you are planning on a local level, however, there is additional work to be done. You must select the markets to advertise in (if you have not done so already) and, more particularly, the stations within those markets that you want to use. That will depend in part on the negotiations that are done by the media buyer. That process is explained more fully in chapter 8.

For cable TV, you may have to rely on broad network information rather than specific programs. Individual cable shows tend to have much smaller audiences (ratings) than do shows on network or spot TV. But those audiences may be more finely targeted due to the nature of this form of television (see chap. 4). Increasingly, cable networks are airing programs multiple times and offering an aggregated rating to advertisers, so that across all showings of an episode of "Biography" on A&E, for example, you will reach 3% of the viewing audience even if that audience is spread across three different airings.

Considerations for Radio Advertising

Radio uses the same principal term as television for planning and buying purposes. That is, you purchase time based on audience ratings. The main difference here is that the rating is based on a time period, rather than on a program. For the most part, you plan radio by dayparts (which were given in chap. 4), although it is possible, for an additional cost, to specify selected, narrower time periods. For example, if you operate a number of McDonald's franchises and only want to advertise in the hour before lunch (which technically falls in Morning Drive), then you could request the noon-to-1:00 p.m. hour, and most stations will sell that time to you, although perhaps at a premium.

Radio audiences are measured by the Arbitron Company, and reported on a quarter-hour basis, so you can look at the average quarter hour (AQH) rating for each station in a market. This is the average number of people listening to an individual station for at least 5 minutes within the quarter-hour period, expressed as a percentage. In many larger advertising agencies, the media planner only specifies the markets to be used, leaving it up to media buyers to choose the actual stations, based on their own knowledge of those markets.

The radio market can be defined (and measured) in several ways. The largest geography is called the *designated market area* (DMA). It is defined as the viewing or listening area in which the counties that have the stations of the originating market get the largest share of household viewing or listening. Every county in the United States is assigned to just one DMA.

A smaller geography for radio is the *total survey area*, which consists of the metropolitan area, plus outlying additional counties that listen to the major metro stations. In Chicago, the total survey area would not only include the Chicago metropolitan area, but also the rest of Cook, Lake, and DuPage counties, which can also receive Chicago radio station signals. The most narrowly defined measure is the *metro survey area*. This is, in fact, defined by government according to the city and surrounding counties that are closely linked economically to the central city area.

The total radio listening figure is provided in the persons using radio (PUR) measure, which is equivalent to TV's persons using television (PUT) number. This tells you what percentage of a given audience listens to radio at a particular time.

If you are purchasing radio time yourself, then a measure that is worth considering is the time spent listening (TSL). This gives an indication of how much time people are spending with an individual station in a daypart, day, or week. The calculation is as follows:

$$TSL = \frac{Number\ of\ quarter-hours\ in\ daypart \times AQH}{Total\ Listening\ Audience}$$

The more time people spend listening to that particular station, the greater the chance of reaching them with your message. On the other hand, if your goal is to reach as many *different* people as possible, then the TSL may be of less concern.

The media specialist should also consider the *cume rating*, which is the total number of people listening to a particular daypart, expressed as a percentage. To find out how quickly a station's audience changes, you can calculate or ask for the audience *turnover* figure, which is the ratio of total number of people listening to a particular station in a daypart to the average number listening to that station in a quarter-hour. If the turnover is high, meaning that people don't listen to the station for very long at any one time, then that would suggest you would need to air your ad fairly frequently in order to reach more people.

An increasingly important area of consideration for radio is merchandising and promotion. Many stations are very willing to organize special contests or announcements, or "added value," events if you buy time from them. If you own a Baskin-Robbins ice cream store, for instance, perhaps you could arrange for the station to hold a contest, with the prize being an ice cream party for the winner and his family. For a local Comcast cable operator, a radio station could agree to air additional announcements and public service messages, in return for being mentioned on the local access cable channel. A Toyota car dealership might provide the perfect venue for the radio station to send some of its disk jockeys on the road for an afternoon, airing the program from the actual showroom. All of these "extras" can be negotiated for little or no additional cost, yet they provide valuable "free" advertising for you and your company. Moreover, because they are organized on a local basis, they help to enhance your firm's place in the community, offering you some image-building public relations too.

For network radio, the terms used are the same, but here you must consider which of the networks to include in the plan. At larger agencies this is often left up to the buyer (where planning and buying are separate functions), based on demographic or format specifications.

Radio audience measurement, which currently relies on samples of people in each market to complete a 7-day listening diary, is moving forward to develop and commercialize a passive means of collecting radio listening activity. Arbitron's portable passive meter (PPM), has been in test markets during the past couple of years. It is a pager-size device worn by a sample of people wherever they go during the day. The meter passively picks up inaudible codes that have been inserted into the broadcast. These codes are used to identify which station was being listened to, by whom, and for how long. In effect, the PPM measures *listening* activity, and does so with far greater accuracy for radio than the listening diary, which requires people to actively remember and write down everything they were tuned to. The technology is able to collect codes from anywhere, including television, sports stadia, or retail stores. Arbitron is using these meters to measure radio listening in 15 different countries outside of the United States. At this time, the PPM is being tested in Houston, Texas. Arbitron is hoping it will become the new currency measurement for radio and, potentially, for other media too.

Considerations for Magazine Advertising

Some of the criteria to consider when planning for magazines include coverage, composition, circulation, subscription, rate base, readership, positioning, and discounts.

Coverage. Just as for the other media forms, the coverage tells you the proportion of a given target group that saw (were "covered" by) the publication in the past month, or whatever is the relevant publication period. The magazine's coverage is similar to a rating in the electronic media.

Composition. This number will show you how concentrated a magazine's audience is with a particular target group. It can be useful in providing the media specialist with some idea of how well the publication will reach your particular audience. If you are advertising baby formula to new mothers, then it would be important to know what proportion of the readers of *Baby Talk* and *Parents* have a newborn. Although the one-page cost or the CPM may be cheaper in *Parents* than in *Baby Talk*, you may reach more new mothers in *Baby Talk* making the cost of reaching one thousand of *those* individuals less expensive.

Circulation. It is important to look at how many copies of the magazine are circulated for each issue. This information is either provided by the magazine itself in an audit report or can be obtained from the Audit Bureau of Circulation, the premier source for circulation data. New or very small magazines may not be audited by this independent organization; if that is the case, be wary of relying on the estimates the publisher provides because they cannot be verified. When looking at circulation, the media specialist should also find out what proportion of that figure is *controlled*, that is, distributed free of charge to potentially interested parties. They are usually not the main target audience for the publication and, therefore, would be less interested in seeing the ads that appear. In addition, you should look at the *net paid* circulation figure, which gives you the number of copies sold at no less than half of the basic newsstand or subscription price. Circulation is usually broken out by geographic area, which can be very helpful, particularly for products that have regional skews.

Subscription or Single Copy. Another valuable number is the percentage of copies sold by subscription versus on the newsstand (single copies). If people are getting their copies sent to them every month, that might suggest they are particularly keen to keep receiving and reading the magazine; on the other hand, the argument could be made that single copy readers renew their commitment to the publication every time they purchase an issue.

Whichever side you believe, it is worth finding out how the subscriptions are sold, and at what price. Publishers used to be able to discount subscriptions very heavily (up to 50%) and still consider them a full subscription. Beginning in 2002, magazines must report the net average subscription price paid by consumers, and reveal the proportion of subscriptions sold at 35% less than that average. This is to counter the belief that, when the price is very low or there are enticing premiums offered to those who buy a year's worth of the magazine, the subscriber is more interested in receiving the free personal stereo or CD than in looking at your ads.

Rate Base.   Finally, you should find out how many times in the past 6 months or 1 year the publisher has not met the guaranteed audience size, or rate base. This is the number of copies that publishers promise the advertiser they will sell. Although the advertiser does not get anything back if that number is not reached, a magazine that consistently fails to meet its rate base is probably one you should avoid. This information is provided by companies such as the Audit Bureau of Circulation that measure circulation on a regular basis. The magazine publisher should also release that data upon request.

Readership.   For those who have access to syndicated services, there is a wealth of additional information available on reading habits for individual consumer magazines. This includes factors such as the average number of days a title is read, the average number of minutes spent with the publication, where it is read, what actions were taken after reading it, and how many readers saw each copy. These qualitative data are summarized in Exhibit 5.4. They may be provided by the individual publication.

Armed with all of this information, the media specialist can then compile a list of preferred magazines to use in the plan. Clearly, the cost of the ad

EXHIBIT 5.4   Qualitative magazine data

Where read
Bought versus obtained
Days spent reading
Time spent reading
Actions taken (e.g., clipped coupon, called toll free number)
Rating of publication
Interest in advertising
Attitudes toward advertising in specific publication
One of my favorites

page will also be a crucial factor in determining which individual titles are selected.

Positioning. There is conflicting evidence concerning where it is best for your ad to be in a magazine. Some studies have shown a clear advantage for being at the front of the issue or on the cover page, whereas others suggest there is little difference in terms of likelihood of being seen. Positioning will also depend on the publication. For some magazines, such as *Cosmopolitan* or *Newsweek,* most of the feature articles appear in the first two thirds of the book. But for more specialized magazines, such as *Network Computing* or *Info World*, readers may also be extremely interested in the smaller ads at the back of the issue that feature products or services for the computer enthusiast.

Discounts. A few years ago, all magazine ads were bought off a rate card that specified exactly how much an ad would cost per issue. Although discounts were given for placing ads in several issues, there was little room for any negotiation. In today's highly fragmented media world, magazines have been forced to become more competitive, both between titles and against other media. One positive result of this, for the advertiser, is that magazines are far more willing to negotiate discounts or special deals now than they were previously. An advertiser who places a large *volume* of ads (and, therefore, dollars) in a magazine will get a special deal, as will advertisers who build up frequency or continuity with the publication. There is also a slight discount for cash payments. It is always worth checking with the magazine's representative to find out if there are ways to lower the unit cost.

Considerations for Newspaper Advertising

If newspapers are to be included in the media plan, the first consideration is which markets are to be used. The list of markets can be developed based on population or household size, on sales data of the product, or on CDIs and BDIs. A list created according to population may be a simple ranking of the markets (top 10, top 20, etc.), or it could be a ranking based on the target audience (top 10 markets where the target is located). Market lists based on sales data will tend to emphasize those places where current sales are occurring, while one derived from CDI or BDI figures will also factor in potential future opportunities.

In looking at the individual markets, the media specialist needs to have a clear understanding of the product's distribution within those areas. Is it available primarily within certain parts of the market, or DMA? Is it found more in the metro area or the suburbs? Are there any major ethnic areas of the market that could play a role in product or media usage?

Once you have determined which markets to use, there are three main criteria to consider for newspaper planning: circulation, coverage, and readership.

Circulation.   As with magazines, the newspaper circulation figure tells you the number of actual copies that are distributed. This figure is used to compare one paper with another, as well as give some idea of how many coupons might potentially be distributed. Circulation is often broken out into counties or city zones, depending on the size of the market. Whereas one newspaper might have a larger overall circulation, another might deliver more readers in the particular zone where your retail outlet is located and therefore be a more appropriate vehicle to use.

Coverage.   The coverage number, also called the newspaper penetration, is the print equivalent of a TV rating. That is, it shows the percentage of households reached by a given newspaper. As with the circulation figure, the numbers might look different depending on how the coverage is defined. Take Boston as an example. If you only consider the overall market, or DMA household penetration, then you might choose the *Boston Globe*, but if you are interested in reaching singles, or Blacks, the *Boston Herald* has greater coverage.

Readership.   Newspaper readership figures provide more detailed information about the paper's readers according to standard demographic breaks or, where available, product usage data. Using these numbers, the media specialist can find out what proportion of the readership is between ages 18 and 49, for example, or how many readers are working women. One newspaper may reach more men than women, or more younger adults than older ones.

The media specialist can use all three criteria to compare different newspapers both within and between markets, as well as help determine which individual papers will do the best job of reaching the given target audience. In markets where there is more than one newspaper available, it is also important to find out how much duplication there is of readers to both vehicles. It could be that one is aimed primarily at the city and the other is read mostly in the suburbs, or that Paper A reaches the northern section and Paper B is preferred in the southern section. Your selection of individual or multiple newspapers will depend to a large degree on the geographic areas that you wish to cover.

Considerations for Outdoor Advertising

As with newspapers, the main decision to be made when including outdoor boards in a media plan is which markets to select. Once that is known, the media specialist must determine which kind of outdoor board to use—poster panels or bulletins. In either case, the unit of sale is the *showing*. It is typically sold as a 25, 50, 75, or 100 GRP showing. The number refers to how many panels or boards are required to reach that proportion of the market. A 50 GRP showing, for example, means that your ad will appear on enough boards to reach 50% of the total population daily. This is completely market specific. Generally, the outdoor company will provide you with the information on how many boards make up each showing size.

Audience delivery estimates are usually also made available by the company that owns the boards, or can be obtained from the Traffic Audit Bureau, which conducts the independent measurement of traffic past those sites. Outdoor billboard measurement in the United States is being revolutionized, thanks to technology. As noted in chapter 4, both Nielsen and Arbitron, the primary TV and radio research suppliers, respectively, have tested new outdoor audience systems that rely on global positioning systems, or GPS, to track consumers as they drive around a city. These satellite systems can pinpoint with far greater accuracy which boards the driver had an *opportunity to see*. Through statistical algorithms, it is then possible to model (approximate) actual billboard exposure, something that was previously unavailable at all. Nielsen has tested this service in Chicago, following its introduction into the South African marketplace. It plans on rolling it out to the top 10 markets in the near future.

Considerations for Internet Advertising

Advertising on the Internet is still developing, so the considerations a media specialist needs to be aware of today may well have changed by tomorrow. But several of the basic considerations are comparable to those of other media.

Position. When Internet advertising was first developed, it didn't matter too much where your ad appeared. It was assumed that it would be enticing and involving enough to attract attention anywhere on the site. Soon, however, advertisers realized that position was as important on the Web as in any other medium. Today, advertisers not only have to select the type of ad to use (banners, buttons, pop-ups, etc.), but also when and where those ads will appear. The cheapest form is run of site (ROS), but most advertisers prefer to pay for a fixed position on a specific page within the site, to have greater control over who will be exposed to that ad message.

Type of Ad. Initially, the most popular kind of ad on the Internet was the banner. This appeared as a rectangle at the top or bottom of the screen or web page. Over time, however, sites introduced a wide variety of alternatives, including the "skyscraper" (going down the left or right hand side of the screen), the button (a small icon or message that links to the advertiser's own site), or an interstitial (a mini-site that appears when the user clicks on the ad). An increasingly powerful form of Internet advertising is search. Here, on Web sites such as Google or Yahoo Search consumers type in what they are looking for on the Internet and a list of possibilities comes up. Advertisers can pay the site to have their product or service appear as a *sponsored link*. Research has shown that, as long as the link is relevant to what consumers are looking for, they will generally not object to the fact that the search result has been paid for.

Metric.   Because the Internet is a more "measurable" medium than any other (except direct response), the metric used can vary. Advertisers can pay for their web ads based on a simple cost per thousand (CPM), or can be more specific and agree to a contract that allows them to pay on a cost-per-click or even cost-per-sale basis.

Considerations for Alternative Forms of Communications

For the myriad of alternative media forms available, the considerations for a planner focus on two key areas: traffic and cost relative to value.

Traffic.   For sponsorships, sporting events, or other location-based opportunities, the planner should try to estimate, in advance, how many people will be in attendance. Even for skywriting above a popular beach, the vendor is likely to know approximately how many sunbathers typically come there on a weekend, for example. Attendance to sports stadiums is easy to capture, as are the number of people at a rock concert or movie theater, if your product is the concert sponsor or is being given away as samples in the theater lobby. Although not a substitute for actual impact, traffic measures at least give an indication of how many people, in theory, will have the opportunity for exposure. For word-of-mouth efforts, the number to determine is how many people could potentially be influenced by the viral efforts.

Cost/Value.   Given that it is not enough for marketers to have their name placed in front of hundreds, or thousands, of warm but disinterested bodies, the planner should also try to assess the value of those expected impressions relative to the cost of obtaining them. Here, it is probably good to consider the contextual relevance of the impact. That is, it might make good sense to have Adidas be a featured sponsor at sports stadiums when soccer matches are played, but less so for a prescription drug such as Paxil to be present at those same events.

SUMMARY

This chapter has covered some of the basic terms and features of media planning. In order to understand media, it is essential that the media specialist be familiar with the concepts of reach, frequency, gross rating points, and gross impressions. Beyond these, it is also helpful to understand the notion of effective frequency, which assumes that in order for an ad to be effective, the target audience has to be exposed to it more than one time. Frequency planning forces you to think about exposure within the purchase cycle. An exposure distribution lets you know the number of people who are exposed a given number of times to an individual vehicle or a complete media schedule. Media costs are accounted for by calculating the cost per thousand (CPM) and cost per rating point (CPP).

The remainder of the chapter looked at various considerations for each major media category. For television, this includes the program rating, audience composition, viewers per viewing household (VPVH). Radio plans need to examine the time spent listening, cumulative rating, and audience turnover. When magazines or newspapers are included in a media plan, it is important to know the publication's circulation, rate base, and actual readership. The main consideration for outdoor is planning the appropriate showing level to reach a given proportion of the target audience with the correct number of billboards. For Internet advertising, the specialist should consider position, type of ad, and measurement metric. Finally, for alternative forms of media, planners should assess the potential traffic for an event or location, as well as the cost relative to the value of the spending.

CHECKLIST—TERMS, CALCULATIONS, AND CONSIDERATIONS

1. Have you figured out how many gross rating points your schedule will deliver?
2. What is the reach, effective reach, and average frequency of that schedule?
3. If you plan to include television in the schedule, have you looked at both program ratings and viewers per thousand viewing household (VPVH)?
4. If you plan to include radio in the schedule, have you looked at the average quarter-hour (AQH) ratings, cume audience, time spent listening, and turnover for each station?
5. If you plan to include magazines in the schedule, have you looked at the coverage, composition, circulation, rate base, ad positions, and discounts?
6. If you plan to include newspapers in the schedule, have you looked at the coverage, circulation, and audience composition figures for each paper?

7. If you plan to include outdoor billboards in the schedule, have you looked at the GRPs available in each market being considered?
8. If you plan to include the Internet in the schedule, have you thought about the ad type, position, and measurement metric you want?
9. If you plan to incorporate alternative media formats in the schedule, have you thought about the traffic to be generated, and the cost of the efforts relative to their impact?

Creating the Plan

Putting together a media plan represents the culmination of all the thinking, planning, and organizing discussed in earlier chapters. That is, with sound advertising and media objectives, a knowledge of who it is we wish to reach with our messages, and a clear idea of what different media can offer us, we are now in a position to start assembling the plan. The key idea to keep in mind when doing this is your *media strategy*. What is it you are hoping to achieve by using media vehicle *X* as opposed to *Y*? How will your combination of media categories and vehicles help fulfill your advertising and media objectives? As with any process, there are several steps to the creation of the plan. These are outlined in this chapter.

TARGET AUDIENCE'S USE OF AND RELATIONSHIP TO MEDIA

The first step in building the media plan is finding out which media your target audience uses and what their relationship is with those media. There is not much point in putting your message about Swiffer mops on hundreds of radio stations across the country if the 25- to 54-year-old adults you are trying to reach tend to be heavy television viewers. You can discover the media habits of your potential customers through syndicated services such as Mediamark Research, Inc. (MRI) or Simmons, or through custom studies that you conduct or solicit on your own. The third alternative, which is the cheapest but may be less accurate, is to do some mini-research on your own. You might want to start asking your clients or customers where they have seen your ads; if you have been advertising in the local newspaper for years but nobody mentions it, then that might indicate the need for a different medium.

By this point, given what you now know about what each media type can offer (and what it can't), you are probably starting to see how the various media will fit in to your particular strategy. So if your goal is to increase awareness of your beauty salon's new manicure and massage treatments, then you might turn to the media best suited to that awareness goal—television and the Internet. On the other hand, if you want to increase the frequency of visits to Pizza Hut restaurant, then local radio might be a better bet because you can place a large number of ads at a reasonable cost and keep repeating the message to remind listeners of that establishment.

Once you think you have a handle on which media are used, then you should consider more closely the *relationship* of those people with their media. This notion, as explained in chapter 2, explores the relationship of consumers to media in order to understand how and why they use the media they select.

For example, the 25- to 54-year-old Swiffer mop users, mentioned earlier, might watch more television than average, according to the syndicated audience measurement data. But, do they do so as an escape from their routines, because they are constantly looking for new information, or because they cannot afford other forms of entertainment? By understanding the target's motivations for media use, the planner will be better able to select the right media types, and vehicles, to communicate the advertiser's message.

As you start to assemble your media categories and vehicles you also need to think about several other considerations—the timing of the plan, its scheduling, and its geographic variations. We consider each of these in the following section.

TIMING OF THE PLAN

For many products, the timing of the plan is self-evident. That is, you want to advertise snowblowers in winter and sunscreen in summer. Other items are tied in to specific days or weeks of the year, such as Valentine's Day candies or Thanksgiving turkeys. But, for the majority of goods and services, you would ideally want to promote them continually, getting your message out on a very regular and frequent basis to reach as many people as you can as often as possible.

There are two obvious drawbacks here. First, for most advertisers, particularly small businesses, they simply cannot afford to do this. And second, there are good reasons *not* to bombard the media constantly with your message. People are going to tire more quickly of your ads, making them tune out or ignore them sooner. They may even grow so irritated by seeing or hearing them all the time that they actually develop less favorable opinions of your brand or company. Most of all, there is no point advertising something unless you have something worth saying. Remember, an advertising message has got to tell consumers about something that will interest them. If all you did was place a message in the paper or on the radio 365 days of the year saying "I'm here," you would be unlikely to see much effect, if any, on your sales.

You need to focus your efforts on particular months, weeks, or days. Deciding when to do so is not all that difficult. Most businesses have some seasonality to them, even those that are used or frequented all the time. You probably know, for example, that people stock up on office supplies at the end of the financial period (quarterly or semiannually); they flock to health clubs at the start of the New Year and when the weather begins turning warmer. Apartment leases tend to be signed in May and October, making the rental business busy just prior to those dates.

You might want to use one of two tactics here. Either you could focus your efforts on promoting your product right before the peak period, reminding people of your existence and trying to take additional share points away from your competitors. Or you could try to build up sales at other times of the year. Or you could try a combination of the two, maintaining a strong presence during the height of your "season," but also keeping a high profile at a couple of other times during the year too. If you do choose to advertise when people may not be thinking about your product, then it is even more important that you tell them something new and interesting. Perhaps you lower your membership rates to the health club in March or October and you announce that in local newspapers and magazines. You need not be confined to "typical" seasonal patterns either. Maybe you can "create" an event for your business. *Cooking Light* magazine sponsors an annual bus tour across the country, promoting the products of its advertisers while offering healthy recipes to those who visit the tour bus. CBS promotes its daytime soap operas through a special mall tour, where some of the programs' stars sign autographs and meet local citizens. These kinds of special events not only provide excellent opportunities for self-promotion in the media, they can also generate additional coverage through public relations efforts and publicity.

It is also worthwhile considering the seasonality of the media you are planning to use. Most media categories have seasonal variations—the fourth quarter is often very tight, for example, because of pre-holiday advertising. For media sold on a supply-and-demand basis (radio and television), this can affect prices considerably. There are only a fixed number of minutes of commercial time available. Even for those media that can expand to accommodate more pages, such as magazines and newspapers, heavy media demand for space during those months may mean it is especially important to place orders well in advance. Other events happen less frequently but have a predictable impact on media buys. Congressional elections every other year, and presidential elections every 4 years, mean that the spring primaries and fall elections can have a significant impact on media availability and pricing in those time periods. In the sporting world, the winter and summer Olympics, alternating with each other every 2 years, affect national media buys around the time of those special events.

BALANCING REACH AND FREQUENCY

As you develop your media plan, it is important to keep track of how well it will perform. That is, you need to keep calculating your reach and frequency measures to compare one potential plan against another. The goal is to find the right medium, or combination of media, that will achieve your media objectives given the amount of money you have to spend. You can do so using the simple calculations shown in chapter 5, based on the size of your target audience and the ratings of the individual media vehicles.

It may turn out that you will not be able to achieve the specific number you set as your goal for reach and/or frequency. In that event, you need to consider several possibilities. It may be that a 55% reach of the target is acceptable, even though you had originally planned to reach 65%, or that a frequency of three is all right when four was the ideal. And, keep in mind that we are dealing here with plan *estimates* rather than actual reach figures. You may be restricted in the actions you can take. If your client demands that his message is seen on television, then that medium must remain in the plan. But perhaps you can opt for cable TV instead of broadcast, and, by reducing the cost, you will be able to place the message more frequently and across more channels, thereby increasing the reach.

Alternatively, you might want to rethink your timing and scheduling strategies. Maybe instead of advertising every 2 weeks for 6 months, you could place your message every week for 3 or 4 months, concentrating your efforts on the most important period and increasing your reach and frequency within that timespan. Or maybe the addition of a third Web site will help boost the numbers by reaching additional target members who are not going to see your ad in the two sites you had first selected.

ROI AND MEDIA MODELS

Whereas media planners should have a good understanding of all the media concepts outlined in chapter 5, today's advertisers and agencies rely heavily on media models to perform the calculations. A media model is a statistical routine performed by computer software packages that goes through the data and manipulates it to project the effectiveness and efficiency of a plan. Various kinds of models are used, all with the overall goal of providing numbers to support the plan. The models are usually based on original numbers of actual audiences to a media type (magazine readership, TV viewership, etc.). They then rely on statistical techniques (e.g., regression) to project out from that data to other demographics, time periods, or markets (depending on the scope of the model).

More recently, marketers have started looking closely at econometric modeling, where statistics are used to try and figure out what marketing (and media) elements are driving actual sales. In so doing, they attempt to measure the media's return on investment (ROI). Although the techniques used are fairly complex, the idea of holding advertising media more accountable for their performance is one that has found favor among high-ranking executives at many corporations. Some find it difficult to believe that any kind of model can truly determine the proportion of sales delivered by any form of indirect and/or brand image advertising (as opposed to truly measurable direct response, promotional, or Internet advertising). But, as marketing budgets are increasingly scrutinized, it is likely that these types of models will only gain in popularity and use.

One problem with ROI is deciding how to define it. For many, it has become synonymous with accountability of media spending. That is, in an increasingly cost-conscious world, marketers want to know precisely what they get back in return for each dollar that they spend in media. The goal is to receive at least $1 of net profit for each dollar that they invest. If they obtain much less than that, then some argue the money is being wasted. Conversely, if the ROI is much higher than $1, it can suggest they are not spending enough because if the advertising and media are having such an impact, then they should be spending more to make the most of that effect. Most accountability studies, however, focus on the short-term impact of the advertising. Did it generate immediate sales of the brand? It is much harder to measure precisely the long-term impact. Let's say your ad for Razor Sharp razors appears in a magazine in one month. Your target does not need any razors for the next 3 months, but in the fourth month, when he is at the store, he sees the product, remembers the ad, and decides he will try it. Many accountability models would not be able to capture that kind of longer term effect.

Another typically unmeasured effect is what is called the *halo effect* of advertising. You might see an ad campaign for Fantastik cleaning spray that talks about how SC Johnson, its manufacturer, cares about keeping families healthy by removing germs from their homes. Your favorable impression of the brand may be transferred to other cleaning products made by the same company, such as RAID or Pledge, even if they are in other cleaning product categories. That "halo" is very hard to capture in statistical models, simply because it is hard to measure. How much of the sales results for Raid, for example, can be attributed to consumers' reaction to the Fantastik advertising?

Indeed, advertising's impact is not always reflected solely in terms of sales. Many brands use the media to convey a message that is designed to improve awareness, enhance brand loyalty, or increase brand consideration. If every ad was supposed to generate an immediate sale, then companies that make cars or computers or other high ticket items would be wasting the vast majority of their ad dollars! Despite these reservations, more advertisers are asking questions about the ROI of their media spending. As a media specialist you may not have simple answers, but you should at least be aware of the discussions going on around the topic.

One of the biggest companies in accountability measurement, Marketing Management Analytics, created a "scorecard" of how accountable each media type is. They gave each medium a rating between 1 and 5 in terms of how easy it was to measure the impact of that medium on consumers. So, for example, they rated outdoor billboards as quite hard, while they considered direct response and the Internet easier to measure for accountability purposes.

SCHEDULING YOUR ADS

You may have a good idea about when to start running your ads. The next question to think about is how to schedule them. Do you want them running each week for 6 weeks (continuity), or twice a month all year (bursts), or for alternating 6-week periods (flighting)? The answer to this question will depend primarily on two interrelated factors: your media objective and your sales pattern. There should always be a timing component stated in your objective, which will give you some guidance for the scheduling of the plan. If you hope to reach 60% of your target during the next 6 months with the message that your hospital was rated the number one pediatric hospital in the city by a *U.S. News and World Report* survey, then you may want to disperse your ads throughout the period to reach as many different people in your audience as possible. H&R Block wants to expose people to its message about its electronic tax filing capabilities, so there would be good reason to schedule most of the ads in the 3 months prior to the April 15 tax deadline, building up the frequency of the message at the time of year when it is most appropriate.

You should also think about the scheduling of different media and their combination. Perhaps you could advertise your Subway store in the local newspaper every week of the year, then supplement it with local cable ads around the time of each special promotion.

Much of what we know about scheduling tactics comes from our general knowledge on reach and frequency. That is, if you wish to reach as many *different* people as possible in your target audience, then you want to disperse your messages across media, vehicles, or days and dayparts, for example. On the other hand, if you want to ensure that your audience hears or sees your ads several times in a given period, then you would concentrate them in fewer media, vehicles, and days or dayparts.

The pattern of scheduling does not seem to make a difference, however, in terms of total reach. So whether your ads appear in two sequential weeks or alternate weeks (one week on, one week off), or are placed 1 week a month over 4 months, the final reach will be approximately the same. Of course, the timing element could be critical, depending on your product. It would not make much sense to spread ads for a highly seasonal item like suntan lotion or Christmas decorations across many months; but, if you are promoting your Charles Schwab office through newspaper ads and on the Internet, then there is something to be said for having a fairly constant presence during the year (perhaps changing the message to tie in to the financial cycle).

Two television scheduling tactics that are sometimes used among major advertisers are *double-spotting* and *roadblocking*. Double-spotting refers to placing two spots within the same program. The effect of this technique is to increase the likelihood of multiple exposure to your ad message (i.e., increased frequency). Roadblocking means placing the same ad across as many channels as possible at the same time, so that when Joe Smith is watching television at 8:06 p.m. on a Friday night, whichever channel he turns to, he'll see the same ad. That is becoming more difficult for advertisers to do as the number of available channels grows higher, making it a much more expensive proposition to undertake. The impact, however, is going to be an increase in reach, because your spot will be seen by Joe and by everyone else who was watching all those channels at 8:06 p.m.

In the 1990s, considerable research was conducted on how best to schedule ad messages to impact sales. A study was done by John Philip Jones that examined the purchase records of households who also had their TV viewing captured via TV set meters (to record what channels were viewed). The results of the study clearly showed that to achieve the greatest "short-term advertising strength" (STAS), the best scheduling tactic was to place at least one message per week across as many weeks as possible. In this way, the plan could impact more people closer to the time of purchase. Although the study had several significant limitations (it only looked at packaged goods, only dealt with television advertising, and only examined households rather than people), its impact was profound. Advertisers began switching their scheduling, moving away from trying to achieve a 3+ reach in a month. Instead, they began looking at a 1+ reach per week, a strategy known as *frequency planning*. Here, the schedule calls for fewer GRPs per week, spread across more weeks of the year. This doesn't make sense in many categories, especially those that require lengthy or high involvement decisions by consumers (cars, houses, financial services), but for many packaged goods manufacturers, frequency planning has now become the norm.

COST-EFFICIENCIES

Costs are obviously very important for the media plan. So, in addition to keeping track of reach and frequency figures as you create the plan, you must also consider the costs involved. Of course, these are closely related. If you need to increase the frequency of your message, it is going to require more media time or space, which means more money. But as already noted,

Exhibit 6.1

		January					February				March			
		2	9	16	23	30	6	13	20	27	6	13	20	27
	Fresh Flakes +Fresh Berry Flakes													
Television	Cable: Prime time	10	10	10	10				10		10	10	10	15
	Broadcast:Prime time													
	Total TRPs	10	10	10	10	0		0	0	0	10	10	10	15
	Total Cost ($000)						$2,500							
Magazines	All Titles													
	Total TRPs						40 TRPs/ month							
	Total Cost ($000)						$950							
Internet	All Sites													
	Total Cost ($000)						$350							
Outdoor	Billboards													
	Bus Shelters													
	Health Clubs													
	Total TRPs													
	Total Cost ($000)													
	TOTAL PLAN TRPs													
	TOTAL PLAN COST ($000)													

Exhibit 6.1 (continued)

		July			August				September			
		17	24	31	7	14	21	28	4	11	18	25
	Fresh Flakes + Fresh Berry Flakes											
Television	Cable Prime time	20	20	25	25	25	20	20	15	15	15	15
	Broadcast: Prime time	50	50									
	Total TRPs	70	70	25	25	25	20	20	15	15	15	15
	Total Cost ($000)		$4,000									
Magazines	All Titles											
	Total TRPs				100 TRPs/ Month							
	Total Cost ($000)				$1,350							
Internet	All Sites											
	Total Cost ($000)				$750							
Outdoor	Billboards											
	Bus Shelters											
	Health Clubs											
	Total TRPs											
	Total Cost ($000)											
	TOTAL PLAN TRPs											
	TOTAL PLAN COST ($000)											

	April				May					June				
3	10	17	24	1	8	15	22	29	5	12	19	26	3	10
15	15			10	20	20	20	15	25	25	25	25	20	20
						50	50	50	50	50	50	50	50	50
15	15	0	0	10	20	70	70	65	75	75	75	75	70	70
				$5,000										
						120 TRPs/ month $500								
								500 $600						
													(continued)	

	October				November				December				Totals
2	9	16	23	30	6	13	20	27	4	11	18	25	
				10	10	10	10						595
													550
0	0	0	0	10	10	10	10	0	0	0	0	0	1145
					$2,500								$14,000
					50 TRPs/ Month $900								
					$200								

it might be possible to find a cheaper medium or vehicle to help your funds go further. Cost-efficiencies can be calculated in terms of cost per thousand of the audience reached (CPM) and through cost per rating points (CPP). These were explained in chapter 5. The more "mass" the medium, the cheaper it will be on a CPM basis, but the less targeted it will be for your situation. That is, there will be a lot of "waste" exposures of people who are probably not interested in what you have for sale. For a widely used product or service, such as car tires or a muffler shop, that might not be a bad thing. But if you are trying to reach a narrower group of people, such as Corvette car owners, to offer them a specially designed luggage rack that sits on the roof of the car, then you would be better off with a higher CPM in a more targeted environment, such as car magazines or car enthusiast Web sites.

TACTICAL CONSIDERATIONS

As you develop your plan, there are probably going to be numerous additional considerations that are specific to your product or service. These might include trade merchandising, consumer merchandising, national-local integration, and testing.

Trade Merchandising

For many goods and services, the trade plays a critical role in the brand's development and sales. Many media plans that are geared primarily to the consumer market also have some side benefits for the trade. When Frito-Lay promotes its Doritos corn chips, it is telling its distributors and retailers that it is pushing the brand and helping to increase their revenues too. A national ad for McDonald's restaurant is also designed to help the local franchisee.

In putting the plan together, therefore, it is important to look at what trade merchandising elements may be attached to it. Perhaps for a chain of Jiffy Lube oil lube shops, you can bring all the operators together for a kick-off party when the media campaign begins. Even something as simple as buttons with your new campaign slogan can help give the trade a sense of being part of the picture. Sending them copies of the new ads and/or materials lets them know what message is being promoted to customers. The media can help here as well, particularly if you are one of their valued customers. They may be willing to co-sponsor an event for your distributors or retailers, for example.

Consumer Merchandising

Although we focus here almost exclusively on advertising media, it is important to keep in mind many of the other ways in which you can gain additional exposure for and mileage out of your media plan. There are a multitude of communications possibilities available, from coupons or sampling to press releases and exhibitions and displays. If you are promoting a line of gourmet preserves, then perhaps in addition to the magazine ads that you run, you can talk to the local grocery stores to set up sampling booths in their stores, and feature the dates and locations in the ads. For an internet services provider (ISP) promoting the latest high-speed Internet access, you could arrange to visit local schools and let the children go on-line, then call the local TV station and arrange for them to film it. The possibilities for these kinds of tie-ins, or integrated marketing, are almost endless. Whatever you do, however, should remain within the overall communications objectives of your plan—increasing awareness, obtaining customer preference, encouraging brand selection, and so on.

To gain as much advantage as possible from consumer promotions, you might also consider increasing other media weight when a coupon is dropped, or placing more newspaper ads the week that you are holding the promotion.

National–Local Integration

Whereas some products (e.g., new movies or product introductions) are advertised solely on a national level, and others (e.g., the local coffeehouse) appear only in local ads, the majority of name brands include both national and local advertising in their media plans. If that is the case, then you need to ensure not only that the message is consistent (something handled by the creative team), but also that the media placements are aligned. There are different ways of doing this. For some, particularly the bigger spending advertisers, the local media weight is added to make an even greater impact on the national spending, such as buying spot TV on top of network, or local newspapers in addition to national ones. For others, typically with smaller budgets, the addition of local media helps to stretch the media dollars further, creating the illusion (in selected markets) that the advertiser has a constant presence. In either situation, you should ensure that there is not unwanted duplication, the messages do not drown out each other to the point of irritating the consumer, and they are not so inconsistent with each other that the consumer is faced with competing messages.

Testing

For smaller advertisers, the notion of testing a plan may seem unnecessary. If you only have a few thousand dollars to spend, then it doesn't seem worthwhile. However, if you are about to change your entire marketing and media strategy, it is a good idea to see first—on a small scale—whether your new approach is likely to increase sales or harm them. For example, Toys R Us, which traditionally advertised primarily in local newspapers to announce whatever was on sale that week or month, changed its strategy to increase awareness of the wide range of items by moving into national television (broadcast and cable). The potential impact of such a media move could be estimated by placing a few of these ads and including some kind of response mechanism, such as a toll-free number or Web site address. That way, the company could test the effectiveness of the TV ads.

Testing is also a good idea for making changes in media weight (GRPs). If you are trying to persuade your client to increase annual spending from a few hundred dollars to several thousand, and you face resistance to the idea, then you might suggest a test of the proposed strategy in one or more markets, to see what impact those added dollars would have to the bottom line.

PRESENTING THE PLAN

Whenever you present your completed plan, whether it is to upper management at your own company or to your client, you need to keep three points in mind. First, *be visual*. Most people either hate or fear media because they believe it is a morass of numbers, most of which they don't understand. So the more you can do to present the information in ways that they can *see* what is going on, the better off you will be. That means using charts, graphs, pictures, photos, or video to liven things up and bring the numbers to life. For instance, if you are presenting the demographic statistics on your target, then perhaps you can make a short video that depicts these people in real life, or present charts or photos that demonstrate who they are.

Second, *be brief*. Although you want to have all of the back-up materials and numbers to support what you are doing, when you make a presentation you should focus on the key points. Assuming you have an interested audience, they will look at the details afterward or ask you questions as you go along. Again, the common perception of media is that it is a mind-numbing experience, filled with mathematical formulas and statistics that are, quite simply, boring.

Third, and perhaps most importantly, *remember the consumer*. Ultimately, your plan is designed to help your client sell more widgets *to the consumer*. So if your plan simply recites a hundred different statistics and presents all of the numbers in charts, tables, and flowcharts, it may be totally accurate but will seem totally removed from the marketing reality that your client lives in.

Fortunately, there are ways around these problems. The first, keeping it visual, can be accomplished through the use of a flowchart. This can, at a glance, show when the ads will run, in which media and vehicles, at what cost, and to what effect (reach and frequency). It can be done for each target in a given plan and can be broken out by medium, if desired. An example is shown later in this chapter. There are numerous ways of creating a flowchart. You can simply draw one yourself, or you can use a spreadsheet computer program or a custom media flowchart package (see Appendix A for details).

Being brief is harder to do. It usually comes down to practice. Running through your presentation with a friend or colleague and asking for their advice can be useful. It is particularly helpful to present your work to someone outside of your area—if they can understand your concise explanations of media terms, then you are doing fine! Remember, however, to include all of the pertinent information (including calculations for how you arrived at your conclusions) in the deck of materials you leave behind. In addition, you have to show how your media plan fits in with and enhances the brand's marketing and advertising objectives and strategies.

Learn as much as possible about the end-user of your product, and include some of those findings in your presentation. You might want to spend some of your own money, for example, to survey some of the customers or do a couple of focus groups to find out how they currently use media and advertising in your category. Include a few of the verbatims (what consumers actually said, in their own words), or even some video of your conversations with customers, to remind your client that you know you are, in the end, dealing with people.

Last but not least, it is crucial to remind your audience that you are dealing with estimates. Some of those may be informed by years of experience, but many are based either on your best judgment, syndicated data sources, or mathematical reasoning. People tend to believe that because you, as the media specialist, have placed a number on something that turns it into "reality." If that were so, media planning would be completely automated and done by rote, a pure science, rather than the combination of art and science that it remains today.

A MEDIA PLAN EXAMPLE

Let's go through an example for a fictitious brand of breakfast cereal, Fresh Flakes. It plans to launch a new line extension, Fresh Berry Flakes, in 2006. It was first introduced in 2000 and competes primarily with Kellogg and Post cereals.

All the data presented here are fictitious.

Situation Analysis

Through the end of calendar year 2005, Fresh Flakes sales are up 3% versus a year ago, a slower rate of growth than seen in the first four years of the brand's existence. It therefore plans to launch a line extension, Fresh Berry Flakes, in June 2006.

Marketing Objectives/Strategies.   Maintain penetration among Fresh Flakes users and launch Fresh Berry Flakes as a new, more exciting addition to the Fresh Flakes line, appealing to existing Fresh Flakes users while drawing new users into the franchise from competitive brands.

The business goal is to increase sales volume of the Fresh Flakes franchise (Original + Berry) by 10% by year-end 2006. It will do so by increasing Fresh Flakes penetration among frequent cereal eaters in two ways:

- Heavy marketing and promotion during launch period and throughout summer months
- Attracting new, especially younger cereal eaters with the Berry Flakes extension

Advertising Time Period: January through December 2006.
Media Budget: $21 million (For Fresh Flakes and Fresh Berry Flakes).
Promotional Activity: Checkout coupons in June-July; product placement on ABC and Lifetime Networks in August-September.

Marketing Background.

Category Competitive Analysis:

- Kelloggs: Total spending: $275 million. 25% network TV; 25% cable TV; 10% syndication TV; 5% Spanish language network TV; 5% spot TV; 15% magazines; 5% Internet; 10% nontraditional.
- General Mills: $250 million. 25% network TV; 30% cable TV; 35% spot TV; 5% magazines; 5% Internet.
- Post: Total spending: $120 million. 10% network TV; 20% cable TV; 45% magazines; 5% Sunday magazines; 10% Internet; 10% nontraditional.
- Quaker: Total spending: $75 million. 40% network television; 20% cable TV; 25% magazines; 5% Internet; 10% nontraditional (sponsorship, placement, etc.)
- Total Category: 20% network TV; 5% Spanish language TV; 25% cable TV; 5% syndication TV; 15% spot TV; 20% magazines; 2% Sunday magazines; 1% newspapers; 2% Internet; 5% nontraditional.

Seasonality: Cereal usage tends to peak in spring/summer months, but the product is used throughout the year.

Fresh Flakes

J/F	M/A	M/J	J/A	S/O	N/D
74	105	126	128	100	63

Cereal Category

J/F	M/A	M/J	J/A	S/O	N/D
92	96	115	118	102	80

Advertising Objective.

1. Generate awareness of the enhanced flavor and taste of new cereal, Fresh Berry Flakes cereal among target with goal of achieving 40% awareness of the brand among the target during calendar year 2006.

Media Objectives.

1. Generate awareness among current users of Fresh Flakes cereal and its competitors. The demographics and psychographics of this target are:

   - Women 18–49, Household income $50,000+
   - Well educated, nutrition oriented, diet/figure conscious
   - The target consists of 15 million women who can be defined as heavy cereal users. They represent 19% of all women.

2. Achieve the following communication goals:

   - *Average 4-week delivery*:

	Reach	Frequency
Women 18–49 with HHI $50,000+	40%	3

3. Provide full year-round media support to stimulate usage throughout year, with additional weight starting in June to support the launch of the brand extension.
4. Schedule advertising run Wednesday–Sunday to complement key grocery shopping days.
5. Provide national advertising support.

Media Strategies

Following the success of the brand during the past 5 years, the 2006 media plan recommends a continuation of the media strategy for Fresh Flakes, using television as the primary medium with magazines as the secondary medium. For the launch of Fresh Berry Flakes, a significant portion of that brand's media dollars will be allocated to outdoor. The Internet will be a prominent part of both brands' plans.

Television.   As the primary medium, television provides:

• High reach/awareness builder
• Sight, sound, and motion
• Immediacy of message
• Targetability (niche networks)
• Continuity (lower cost cable networks)
• Added value programs (product placement, contests, etc).

The following cable networks are more likely to be viewed by the target:

• E! Entertainment
• MTV Networks
• Comedy Central
• Food Network
• Nick-at-Nite
• HGTV

One quarter of the television weight will be in broadcast prime time for the launch of Fresh Berry Flakes.

• Prime time offers higher ratings, greater reach

Magazines.   As the secondary medium, magazines provide:

• Long message life
• Repeat exposure
• Targetability—ability to provide contextually relevant and engaging message
• Editorial compatibility
• Inserts (coupons, advertorials)

Magazines will be divided between health and fitness (30%), fashion and beauty (20%), entertainment (20%), and food (30%). Most magazine ads will be 1P4C (one-page, four-color). For the Fresh Berry Flakes launch, 1 1/3 pages will be added in selected titles. Preferred positions will be:

• Health and fitness: Fitness section

- Fashion and beauty: Fitness section
- Entertainment: News section
- Food: Front of book

The recommended magazines will include:

- *Cosmopolitan*
- *Entertainment Weekly*
- *Essence*
- *Martha Stewart Living*
- *Self*
- *Glamour*
- *Marie Claire*
- *Cooking Light*
- *Bon Appetit*
- *Fitness*

Internet.   A combination of portals, Web sites, and key word searches will be utilized. The following sites and portals will be included:

Portals	*Sites*
Yahoo Health	Cookinglight.com
AOL Health	Fitness.com
Google (search on health, fitness, cereal, breakfast, diet)	Self.com

All Web site ads will be rich-media, and use behavioral targeting to come up based on the pathways taken by users.

Outdoor.   A combination of outdoor billboards, bus shelters, and health club advertising will be used during the Fresh Berry Flakes launch period (June–August). The advantages of outdoor include:

- Broad reach, particularly to mobile younger population
- Target selectivity (e.g., health clubs)
- Multiple exposure/high frequency

The flow chart on pp 140–141 depicts how the plan would be laid out during the year.

Although this is a very generalized and simple version of what to include in a plan, it provides the basic information that has been covered earlier in this book. You should note that all of the recommendations need to be backed up by research data, wherever possible, beyond simple tables showing indices or coverage for individual media vehicles or gross expenditures for the year. Here is a brief list of the kinds of analyses that could be included in the "back-up" for this plan:

- Media usage
- Cable TV network comparisons
- Magazine comparisons
- Web site comparisons
- CPM comparisons (e.g., cable vs. broadcast vs. online)
- Daypart/program rankings by target
- Detailed reach and frequencies by medium
- Media quintiles
- Purchase volume for brand and category
- Demographic/lifestyle analysis of users
- Brand geographic analysis (BDI vs. CDI by DMA)
- Seasonality analysis
- Grocery shopping patterns
- Historical media plans

SUMMARY

When creating a media plan it is crucial to consider first the target audience's use of media, in terms of which categories and vehicles they use. You then must determine the plan's timing, if there are seasonal sales or other elements of the marketing mix (pricing, promotion, distribution or product changes) that will affect the plan's timing. For scheduling of your chosen vehicles, financial considerations and reach and frequency goals will help determine when, and how often, your ads appear. Tactical elements are important, too, particularly trade and consumer merchandising, to receive maximum support from dealers, distributors, and retailers, and maximize the impact of the advertising. If funds permit, or major changes to the plan are being contemplated, it is recommended that the plan be tested on a small scale before being launched in its entirety.

CHECKLIST—CREATING THE PLAN

1. Have you found out as much as possible about your target audience, either through syndicated services or primary research you have conducted?
2. Have you determined the appropriate timing for your messages?
3. How will your messages be scheduled—continuously, in flights, or in bursts?

4. Will your reach and frequency goals be met by your timing and scheduling strategies?
5. Are there merchandising possibilities for your brand with either the trade or with consumers?
6. Do you need to test the plan first in a smaller location before rolling it out?
7. Can you present your plan in a visually interesting and succinct fashion?

CHAPTER 7

Offering Alternatives

Once you have completed your media plan, you might think your task is over. But like the Energizer bunny in the popular battery commercials—created in the early 1990s, and reintroduced periodically thereafter—it keeps going, and going, and going. In fact, even as you are creating the plan, you should be starting to think about various alternatives. Although you might be convinced that you have created the perfect, biggest sales-generating, best objectives-meeting media plan ever conceived, the chances are fairly good that it will not be accepted at face value. So rather than going into your presentation believing that your job is over and the client will immediately accept everything you are recommending, you will be in a much stronger position if you prepare some alternatives beforehand. This chapter considers some of those options.

SPENDING MORE MONEY

The opportunity to gain a larger budget than you were originally expecting does not happen very often, and certainly not as often as a media specialist might like! However, there are several good reasons for being prepared to spend more on advertising media than was originally proposed. The first, from an agency perspective, is that if you are being paid a commission on the media you buy, the more money you spend, the more you will make. But second, and perhaps more importantly today when fewer advertisers are paying a 15% commission rate, it is your job as the media specialist to prove to the client how much more effective the media plan *could* be if there were more dollars available.

Some people might find this purely wasteful. There is evidence, after all, to indicate that spending more on advertising may actually result in a *decrease* in

140

sales! But, for the most part, research supports the notion that placing more dollars in advertising media to reach more people on more occasions (assuming, of course, they are the right people for your product) will increase sales. That won't occur in a vacuum; the other "Ps" of the marketing mix have to be working in your favor too. The product must be one that the marketplace needs, there has to be good distribution, and the price must be appropriate. But given those factors, increasing media dollars will tend to increase sales.

So, given those circumstances, how do you best prepare to offer the alternative of spending more? In many situations, the best way is to simultaneously create a second media plan that has a larger budget allocated to it. If your primary plan has an annual media budget of $2 million, then you might consider creating an additional one at the $3 million level to see how that would perform. In doing so, you should not simply throw extra media weight around randomly. Instead, you should revisit your advertising and media objectives and consider what you might set as your goals if you had that extra money to spend. If, for instance, your original goal was to boost awareness of the latest Best Buy store to open in Chicago, then perhaps if your budget was to be 20% larger, you might think about setting your objectives higher also, proposing that with the additional funds you could increase awareness to 40% in that same time period.

Another option with increased funding is to disperse your message across a wider area. If you have coffee stores located primarily in three states, but are starting to expand into five additional states, then perhaps by spending more money on advertising media you could afford to put your messages into those new areas to let people know of your upcoming presence. Having more money might also allow you to branch out into additional media vehicles or forms. If your basic media plan for Tropicana Orange Juice for kids consists of network television and magazine ads, then perhaps the extra dollars could be spent on radio or Internet ads.

Of course, in suggesting where and how this extra money could be spent, you must always show what will be achieved in return. That is, you need to quantify, wherever possible, the positive impact those dollars will have. This can be done through reach and frequency calculations that show how many additional people in the target will be reached, and how many more times they will have the opportunity to be exposed to the message. Supplementary funds may also end up *lowering* the cost of individual ads, either through volume or frequency discounts, or by reducing the cost per thousand (CPM). So although the bottom-line cost of the plan may go up, the cost efficiency may actually improve.

Another advantage to spending more media dollars is that they may allow you to reach a secondary target more readily. If you are putting a plan together for the Beef Council, where the primary target audience is women who like to cook, then perhaps expanding the plan will allow you to address more clearly a secondary target audience of restaurant chefs. You might also think about using additional dollars to reach people who can influence your primary target. For a media plan aimed at parents offering a college fund, you might spend the extra monies to promote your company to financial planners to whom the parents will turn for advice.

It is also important to think beyond media when considering how additional dollars might be spent. You might want to recommend undertaking some custom research of your proposed target audience, especially if that target has changed in some way from previous plans. Or research could be done to gain a greater understanding of how the target you are trying to reach uses the media in your plan, or where they turn to for information about the product or service that could, in turn, greatly enhance your media plans in the future. The latter could be particularly valuable if there is very little syndicated data currently available, or if you are in a very specialized or new field, such as biotechnology or wireless web devices.

And, of course, the people who actually create the ads would also like to have more money to spend on their work. Production quality could be improved, commercials lengthened, or better talent hired if more dollars were made available. You could make your direct mail piece look far more professional, or enhance the design on your Web site, or distribute more samples to individuals visiting your exhibit at a trade show. The possibilities are almost endless. But whatever you recommend for your increased-spending scenario, you must justify it in terms of the objectives and strategies that you have stated upfront (even if you propose modifying those objectives if you get additional funds).

SPENDING LESS MONEY

Unfortunately, for most media specialists, the more common case is that you will end up having to spend less than originally proposed. And although it is generally not a good idea to present to your client or boss a reduced-spending alternative at the same time as you present your main media plan (unless that has been specifically requested), you would be well advised to start thinking about how you would spend less money as you are developing the basic plan.

There are numerous reasons why you might end up having less money than you anticipated available for your plan. It could be that sales of Pepperidge Farm cookies fell more than expected this year, so marketing budgets for the coming year had to be cut (and, remember, advertising is usually the first item to be cut when sales go down, despite the fact that those dollars will typically help *increase* sales). New management or ownership will often result in budgetary changes, and again, more often than not these changes are in a negative direction. It could be that the company decides to speed up the introduction of a new brand and decides to take money away from the established product for which you are preparing a plan. Or the marketer has decided to deliver a corporate message featuring all of its brands in one ad, reducing the amount to be spent on the plan.

Whatever the reason, as you are preparing an alternative plan, think carefully about how you can put together a media schedule that will come as close as possible to meeting your original objectives. There may be several ways to cut corners without decimating the plan. Perhaps you can shorten the flight times, running TV ads for 2 weeks at a time instead of 4, or cut the number of Web sites you are on, or only place ads in magazines every other month instead of monthly.

Many advertisers today are pulling dollars out of regular national television and switching it into product placement deals that have a lower out-of-pocket cost. Both General Motors and Procter & Gamble spent less in the 2005 network TV upfront buying season and switched those funds to "alternative" media, including product placement. P & G's Crest toothpaste, placed in "The Apprentice," generated more than 3 million Web site hits in one day. A total of $4.25 billion was expected to be spent in this non-traditional advertising form in 2005, up 23% from the year before. In the 2004–2005 television season, there were about 7,500 product placements captured in prime time in the six broadcast networks. This activity was not undertaken by a handful of advertisers; rather, more than 1,500 of them placed their brands within the programs themselves.[1]

Creating a reduced-spending scenario should not be a case of simply cutting spots or pages arbitrarily. It must be done with strategic reasoning in mind. For instance, let's say you have a media plan to get more parents in your area to consider sending their children to your client's preschool program, but instead of having $300,000 to spend, you end up having only $240,000. You had originally intended to send direct mailings to all parents of young children in the vicinity, inviting them to visit the school, as well as placing newspaper ads in community papers. Now, with less money to spend, you must reconsider how best to allocate your dollars yet still achieve your objective. Perhaps instead of using direct mail, which tends to be very expensive, you could try to get free publicity by sending a video news release to the local TV stations and media kits to other local media. An open house would be an inexpensive way of offering parents the opportunity to visit the school. In addition, getting your school's Web site up and running, and linked to local or regional sites that deal with education, would also be fairly simple and inexpensive. But, in order to reach a broad cross-section of people, sustaining a minimum level of newspaper ads would probably remain an efficient and effective approach.

---

[1]Nielsen Media Research, 2005.

When considering which ads or insertions to remove, you must also keep in mind that a reduction in frequency may result in the loss of some volume discounts with the media involved. Reducing the number of places your message appears in or on will also impact your reach. So reductions will likely mean you come up short on your reach and frequency goals.

Sometimes there is no alternative but to cut one or more media forms from the plan. Before doing so, it is important that you consider each one in turn, deciding what would be the result of eliminating that medium on the overall plan's objectives. This should not be limited to reach and frequency considerations, but also thought of in terms of what the medium can do for your ad and how important that medium is in consumers' lives. If you take out all TV from a plan, then remember that you are losing a key medium that offers sight, sound, and motion and the opportunity to deliver the message to a large audience. That might be less important for a Ford dealership, but critical for a Red Lobster restaurant where you want to showcase the food. It also depends on how consumers relate to their media. For example, if you know from your communications planning research that your working mother target for Welch's juice boxes has a strong relationship with magazines, then removing them from your plan, even if they represent a higher CPM, is likely to be detrimental to the plan's impact and its ability to engage your audience.

Another way to reduce media spending is to use briefer or less expensive ads. Instead of 30-second commercials, maybe you could make do with half that time; instead of a full-page ad, perhaps a half-page ad will suffice. Once again, however, this must be considered not simply in numerical terms (e.g., reach, or CPM), but also in terms of the impact on consumers seeing or hearing that commercial message. Although some research evidence suggests that many consumers cannot tell the difference between a 15-second and a 30-second commercial, there is obviously less time available in the shorter unit to tell the complete story, so you are missing out on the chance to reinforce your message as thoroughly.

It might seem appropriate, given a reduced media budget, to cut the size of your target audience and plan to reach fewer people. In fact, in many situations that can turn out to be *more* costly, because the more narrowly you try to target your media, the more expensive it becomes to try and reach them. If your original plan for a new Pillsbury cake mix is aimed at all women from age 18 to 49 and uses a mix of magazines and TV, then by trying to narrow it further to reach only those women in that age group who have household incomes of more than $75,000 and have three or more children you will probably end up looking at more expensive media vehicles. Instead of picking a broadly popular woman's service magazine, such as *Good Housekeeping* or *First for Women,* you might end up with magazines that have a smaller circulation and cost more per ad page, such as *Gourmet* or

Bon Appetit. Now admittedly, they *will* reach more of your more narrowly defined target, but the cost may be correspondingly higher, too.

One way you could consider making cutbacks on your targets is by eliminating any secondary targets you had planned to reach through separate media. A plan that was intended to increase awareness of an environmentally friendly detergent might be aimed at both environmentally aware consumers and opinion leaders. Faced with a cutback in media dollars, you might consider targeting only one of those groups initially, rather than both of them at once.

It is extremely important to outline the implications and results of spending less on advertising media. This should not be done in a gloom-and-doom fashion, portraying a picture of complete failure if $50,000 is removed from the budget, but neither should it be taken lightly and happily accepted without a fuss. If for no other reason, explaining what you believe might happen if those media dollars are removed will show to your client that you have thought through in a strategic way the possible outcomes of alternative plans. Keep in mind that your ultimate goal is to get those media dollars restored as soon as it is feasible to do so.

CHANGING TARGETS

Sometimes after you have presented a complete media plan to the client and have apparently won approval for it, a little voice in the back of the room will speak up and say, seemingly casually, "But what would happen if we targeted X instead?" That simple sentence can send the alarm bells flashing and blood pressure soaring for the media specialist. It is important not to panic at that point, but rather to think carefully about whether or not there is real merit to the question.

First of all, you must ensure that the media target is in line with the brand's marketing target, otherwise it will be hard for the media plan to fully achieve the overall marketing objectives. Although you may feel indignant that anyone is questioning your plan's target, particularly after all the work you have put into it, you need to step back and take a careful, considered look at the proposition. For as much as you may be reluctant to admit it, it could be that the person making the suggestion has actually hit on a potentially valuable target that you had simply not considered or thought to be very important. Sometimes it takes so long for the client and agency to agree on a single target that once a definition has been pinned down, there is a tendency for the media specialist to put on the blinders and work feverishly to deliver a plan with the agreed-on target. Any considerations of alternatives have been set aside out of gratitude that the client has finally accepted at least one customer group. But as you are increasingly wrapped up in that target audience, the client may have time to sit back and ponder other possibilities, and may come up with one that is more appropriate, or equally so.

In the best scenario, that alternative target *is* in fact one that you had considered and rejected, either because of strategic or financial reasons. You can then explain why the different target would not be appropriate or feasible. If you had not already done so, then it is in everyone's interest to look more carefully at the proposed alternative (unless it seems so outlandish and unreasonable that you are certain there is no merit to it). It could be that a simple discussion then and there will be enough to determine whether this option should be investigated further. Or, you may have to go back to syndicated research or whatever sources you were using to define the target and examine the proposed alternative more closely.

There are other situations where it is incumbent on you, as the media specialist, to consider different targets as you are developing the primary plan. As already noted, this could be because you are creating alternative spending scenarios with more or fewer dollars available. But it might also arise because of disagreement or uncertainty over the best target for the product. Perhaps your bank client has always targeted its media plan to promote its mortgages at young couples looking for their first home. You, as the media specialist, might put together a second plan that targets older couples whose children have left home who want to move to a smaller, but more elegant, home for their retirement, or are perhaps contemplating buying a second weekend home. Clearly, the media that you would use to reach each target group would be very different.

It could also be important to include different targets in a plan, or to create a separate plan for those targets when you think that there are critical secondary audiences who need to be addressed. This is highly dependent on the product category. For medicines or health care items, for example, it is often essential to communicate with the medical profession as well as consumers, because they are the ones who influence which brands are selected. With the removal in the late 1990s of restrictions on television advertising of prescription drugs, there has been an enormous increase in the amount pharmaceutical companies are spending on that medium. Even though consumers must still ask their doctors to prescribe these specialized drugs (e.g., Prozac, Paxil, or Lipitor), the advertising is aimed at influencing the consumers to ask their physicians for a specific brand-name medication, rather than simply something to help with depression, arthritis, or allergies. More recently, there have been calls for such pharmaceutical advertising to be re-regulated out of concern that the ads are working too well, encouraging doctors to prescribe more drugs (and more name-brand drugs) than they would otherwise have done. Merck went as far as announcing that it would refrain from consumer ads for any new product that it launched for the first year the drug is in the marketplace.

Another area where critical secondary audiences exist is with children's products. When they are targeted, it is frequently advisable to have a separate target of moms or parents because they typically hold the purse-strings. It is estimated that children influence tens of billions of dollars worth of spending each year. In many countries around the world, there are strict limits on which products, and how products, can be advertised directly to children, out of concerns that they are more easily misled by advertising.

Whoever the different target is, the media specialist must determine which different media are needed to reach those people. That, in turn, will depend on the marketing and advertising objectives for that distinct audience: Are they identical to the main target's goals, or do they differ in some way? How much do the two targets overlap, both in terms of those objectives and in their media usage patterns? It could be, for example, that if you are trying to encourage both consumers and contractors to select your Grohe faucets, then certain ads placed in home decorating magazines would reach both groups, but more specialized trade publications will do a better job at convincing contractors of the merits of your brand, whereas TV ads could help enhance your brand's image among consumers.

CHANGING MEDIA

As the media specialist, your job really entails considering different media from the beginning to the end of media plan development. You are doing so as you assess your media strategy and tactics and as you create the plan. However, it is sometimes worthwhile to make a special effort to consider how the plan would turn out if different media were used. Again, this could be in reaction to a change in the media budget, or a response to a client's question. Or you could take it upon yourself to investigate alternative media options.

In some cases, this could involve looking at different media vehicles within the same media form. If you are recommending magazines, then perhaps you might look at more specialized publications to reach your target. For TV, reconsider whether you should use broadcast, spot, or cable TV to convey your messages, or maybe even switch to product integration. With a radio plan that uses spot markets, perhaps a network buy would be more efficient and appropriate. With Internet buys, you may want to think about whether to buy ads on broad-based portals (Yahoo, MSN, etc.) or pay to be a sponsored link on a search page. If your media plan makes heavy use of newspapers, then think about whether you should move from small town local newspapers to those that are distributed across broader regions, such as the *Boston Globe* in the New England area, the *Chicago Tribune* in the Midwest, and the *Los Angeles Times* in California.

The use of different media vehicles will depend primarily on two factors: cost-efficiency and targetability. It may be cheaper to use cable rather than spot TV, for instance, but if cable penetration in your area is only at 60%, then you are missing out on the 40% of the homes who could potentially be exposed to your message. Switching from smaller local papers to bigger, more regional ones may bring you a larger audience, but those people may not be close enough to your chain of Chipotle Grill casual Mexican restaurants to be worth reaching with your message.

The bigger change when thinking about different media is a switch in media forms altogether. Instead of recommending newspapers, what happens if you use local cable TV instead? How about using the Internet instead of magazines? Or what would be the result of switching dollars out of magazines and into television? And how much would that change be affected by the relationship of your target with the media you are considering? The media specialist must think through these scenarios both from the point of view of strategy and of cost. How would a move from newspapers to cable TV affect your overall objective of boosting awareness of your health food store? Would the same number of people be reached? Would they be the same people? What is the cost difference? And how would message frequency be impacted? What are the creative implications of such a change? All of these questions need to be answered as you develop a plan using different media.

One of the tools used in helping determine alternatives for a plan is the optimizer. Developed in the United Kingdom in the 1980s, these computer systems were first designed to select the optimal mix of national TV dayparts or types against a specific target. They use algorithms that balance the reach of a plan against its cost to arrive at a solution that maximizes one or the other (cost or reach). Although they are models based on historical data (ratings), they are now routinely used predictively to help media planners and buyers determine what TV dayparts or specific programs to include. Following their introduction, multimedia optimizers were created that include television, radio, and print, although with varying degrees of success, due to the fact that the ratings data for each medium are collected and reported differently.[2]

The main idea to keep in mind when offering media alternatives is that your original plan is not the only way to schedule media to meet your client's marketing and advertising objectives. Here again we see that media planning is both art and science. There are potentially tens, if not hundreds, of different ways that you could plan your media to obtain the designated goals. Your job as the media specialist is to come up with the one that you believe will do the most effective and efficient job, while fully understanding that there are alternatives available that might achieve the same ends.

---

[2] "Point of View: Optimizers and Media Planning," Erwin Ephron, *Journal of Advertising Research*, vol. 38, no. 4, July/August 1998, 47–56.

TESTS AND TRANSLATIONS

There are two common ways to conduct tests of a media plan on a local or regional basis. They are known as *As It Falls* and *Little America*. Here, we consider the basic concepts for each one, rather than going through all of the mathematical calculations needed to prepare such a plan. Although this procedure is really a test, it is also sometimes referred to as a "test translation" to reflect the fact that a national or bigger plan is being recreated in some fashion on a smaller scale. And even though, as media specialists, we are most concerned with testing the media plan itself (increasing GRPs, trying different scheduling strategies, etc.), tests are also often conducted to determine the impact of new creative, or to see how a new product fares in the marketplace.

As It Falls

This type of test is most often used for brands in existing product categories, where the competitors are well known. The main premise of this method is that the rating points are allowed to occur as they normally would in each market, or *as it falls*. So rather than have the same GRPs across all test markets, the plan's goals would vary somewhat from location to location, depending on how well the individual vehicles perform in each place. That also means that the budgets will vary by market too. It may cost $5,000 to buy 100 radio GRPs in Boise, Idaho, but it may cost $10,000 to get the same GRP level in Madison, Wisconsin. The main advantage to this testing system is that it provides a realistic scenario for assessing the impact of the test plan. If the plan were expanded to a national level, there would still be market-by-market differences similar to those seen in the as-it-falls test situation.

Little America

This test market procedure is used more often with new brands or products where there is no existing competition. What it sets out to do is recreate a national plan in one (or a few) markets, or get as close to that as is feasible. It usually involves more complex planning, first to determine how individual media categories perform in the markets you choose, and then to figure out how to adjust the test plan so that it matches the national delivery.

SUMMARY

While creating a media plan, the true media specialist is already considering various alternatives. One that should always be included is a "what-if" scenario of the effect on the plan's outcome if more dollars were available, looking at the impact on cost efficiency, reach, and frequency, and the marketing and advertising objectives. Increased funding could also be allocated to gain additional reach of the brand against its users, or improved production quality of the ads themselves. This chapter also examined a reduced-spending scenario, which must be undertaken with a strategic focus in mind, considering alternative media forms or vehicles, or fewer messages or targets. Indeed, plan alterations will frequently look at different targets or different media and estimate the impact those might have on the plan's effectiveness and its ability to engage consumers with your brands' messages through the right media. All of these potential changes can be tested by translating the plan into a local or regional test market situation and seeing what happens there first.

CHECKLIST—OFFERING ALTERNATIVES

1. Have you prepared a second media plan at a higher budget level?
2. Have you considered how extra funds would be spent—longer flights, wider geographies, secondary targets—and how those would impact your media (reach and frequency) goals?
3. Are there nonmedia needs that require additional funds (creative requirements, consumer research, trade allowances)?
4. Do you know the impact of spending fewer media dollars on your plan—(fewer media categories or vehicles, reduced number of targets, reduced schedule, lower reach and frequency results)?
5. Are there other target audiences you should consider?
6. Are there other media categories to be considered?
7. Is it necessary to test your media plan first, either "as it falls" (existing brands) or in a "little America" (new products) test?

CHAPTER 8

Making the Media Buys

Even the most impressive media plan will not satisfy the client until the time and space have actually been bought. The role of the media specialist may involve none, some, or all of the media buying functions. This chapter provides a brief overview of how print and electronic media are purchased. The subject really requires book-length treatment on its own; the goal here is to show how media buying fits in with the planning process, rather than explain the many details and intricacies of the buys themselves.

MERCHANDISING A MAGAZINE BUY

It is fairly common in many smaller or midsize advertising agencies for media planners to be responsible for magazine buys, although at larger agencies there is usually a specialized staff of print buyers who focus solely on the negotiations. It used to be that all magazines worked off a *rate card*, listing the cost of buying various page sizes, with or without color or other special features. Additional charges were also made for preferred positions, such as the inside front or back covers and the back cover itself, which are believed to be read by more people.

Although the extra costs remain, today's magazine buys are far more likely to be made by negotiating. That is, the rate card is usually the starting point, but then it is up to the media specialist and the magazine's representative (or rep) to discuss the final cost for the client. Discounts may be offered for volume buys if, for example, the client purchases ads in multiple issues, or buys several pages in one issue, or increasingly, buys space in several magazines owned by the same publisher. As we learned in chapter 3, the cost of a magazine ad will depend on the size and nature of the magazine's readership. Obviously, you will pay more to reach more people. It would cost you about $213,000 for a full-page, 4-color ad in *Ladies Home Journal,* which has a circulation of 4.1 million, whereas the same ad placed in *Vanity Fair,* which has a circulation of 1.1 million, will cost less than $110,000.

At the other end of the spectrum, however, you may also have to pay more to reach a highly specialized audience. Although both *First for Women* and *Bon Appetit* have circulations of 1.3 million, the one-page ad will cost $52,000 in the former and $92,000 in the latter because it is assumed that the more focused material of articles about food is reaching a more interested, involved audience that is more likely to pay attention to the ads in that publication. There have been research studies both supporting and rejecting this hypothesis, with the dissenters claiming that if readers are more involved in the subject matter, they are in fact *less* likely to pay attention to the ads. For the media specialist, the main focus should be on the suitability of each individual magazine to the media objectives, and how efficiently and effectively each vehicle can be used.

When the magazine space is negotiated, the specialist will usually request certain positioning preferences. As already noted, for some of these a premium must be paid. Aside from covers, the specialist may want a Kraft cheese ad, for example, placed near or within the food editorial, or a Cover Girl cosmetics ad to appear in that section of the magazine. Sometimes it is enough to simply request that the ad is in the first third of the issue, under the assumption that those pages are more likely to be seen. The willingness and ability of the magazine to fulfill these requests will vary, depending on who the client is and how many ad pages it needs to fill. One of the important things to remember about magazines is that, unlike electronic media, which have a finite amount of airtime, printed media (including newspapers) can simply add pages if they can attract additional advertisers.

In addition to the increased willingness of magazines to negotiate off the rate card, more publications are also offering additional benefits to their advertisers. These might include special promotions, editorial features, bonus circulation, web links, or trade deals. These are usually offered at little or no extra charge, but obviously the cost is built into the amount the specialist pays for the ad pages. These extras reflect the extremely competitive media landscape, with an increasingly fragmented marketplace not only within the magazine industry, but also across different media. *Good Housekeeping* does not only compete with the other women's service books (*Better Homes and Gardens, Ladies Home Journal, Family Circle,* and *Woman's Day*), it must also fight for dollars with television, radio, newspapers, outdoor billboards, direct mail, the Internet. The list is almost endless.

Once the magazine space has been agreed on, in terms of price, special features, and positioning, it is time to make the actual buy. At larger agencies this is accomplished through a magazine authorization, which sets out the terms of the contract to which both parties must agree. Some clients may like to see this first to be sure they know what they are getting. If everyone accepts these terms, then the media specialist can go ahead and authorize the buy.

GETTING NEWS INTO NEWSPAPERS

The purchase process for newspapers is similar to that of magazines. First, buyers must analyze all possible newspapers available in each designated market, looking at factors such as circulation, coverage, audience composition, color possibilities, and zoning (the ability to customize ads to different areas of the paper's coverage area, or only appear in selected editions). Thanks to technological advances, newspaper ad inserts can be distributed in a more targeted fashion than previously. Today, most newspapers can vary the inserts by zip code.

Then, they must negotiate with each newspaper to obtain the best rate. Newspapers are purchased in terms of standard ad unit sizes (SAUs), so that although the size of the newspaper itself may vary, its ad sizes are standardized. Just as with magazines, the newspaper buyer will usually want to specify the section of the paper in which the ad will appear—an ad for Hellman's salad dressing in the food section, an ad for Universal Studio's latest movie in the entertainment section, and an Ethan Allen furniture store ad in the home section. Sometimes, that decision is made based on what the target audience is more likely to read, so an ad for Verizon's PDA service might appear in the business section to reach professionals who are more likely to be interested in that item.

Once the deal has been negotiated and agreed on, an insertion order is placed with the newspaper. At the same time, the agency will issue a Newspaper Authorization that sets out all of the specifications for the ad, such as whether it will be black and white or color, whether or not it includes a coupon, and if there are any special instructions. Then all the print details must be confirmed, including the insertion dates, closing dates, ad size, column inches, inch rate, gross cost, contract rate, and position in the newspaper. This is done for every newspaper in which the ad will appear. After that has received approval, the insertion order goes ahead and the buy is made.

BUYING TIME ON TELEVISION

There are three ways that national television is bought, for both broadcast and cable TV and syndication—long term, short term ("scatter"), and opportunistic. The first, and most intense, is what is generally known as the "upfront" marketplace. This usually takes place for broadcast TV in late-May after the networks present their new programming slate to advertisers, whereas for cable it runs from May to July. With either television form, the media specialist negotiates time with the major networks well in advance of the actual air dates. Most typically, these fall during the following TV season that starts in September and runs through to the following May. The time purchased is usually over three to four quarters of the year.

When TV advertising was initiated in the late 1940s, all commercial time was, in effect, bought "upfront". That is because programs were fully sponsored by advertisers, so the negotiations for which companies would put their names in front of new programs' names occurred as those same programs were being developed (the Philco Theater Hour). After quiz show scandals in the late 1950s, where contestants were secretly fed the right answers in order to maintain viewer suspense, the networks took back control of programming from advertisers (who had sponsored those unfair quiz shows). In 1962, ABC became the first TV network to air all of its new programming in one week, right after Labor Day, and the "new fall season" was born. From then on, the annual schedule was born. The network marketplace is a modified version of supply and demand, with TV ratings (viewers) acting as the supply, and advertiser budgets providing the demand. However, given that the networks have certain profit goals to meet, they will only offer programs at a price that is in line with those goals, therefore diminishing the dynamics of a true supply-and-demand market. In 1967, ABC also became the first network to offer the "guaranteed" program rating, to advertisers who agreed to buy upfront. Although this meant the advertiser had to commit to a buy in advance, the advantage was that "hit" programs might be purchased at a relatively inexpensive cost. Today, upfront buys account for from 80% to 85% of all network prime-time sales. In 2004, about $9.2 billion worth of network TV ad time was sold this way.[1]

When you buy *long-term*, you receive a guaranteed rating, along with the opportunity to set up cancellation options. Typically, the options decelerate over the future quarters. For instance, in the first quarter, you might buy all of the spots confirmed; in the second quarter, three quarters, or 75% might be firm, with the option to cancel the remaining 25% by an agreed-on date. Then for the third or subsequent quarters, only half of the spots you negotiate are firm, and half (50%) are cancellable by a certain date. One advantage of buying time this way is that more favorable rates may be offered up front, because the networks like to lock in the advertisers to their shows (both new and returning series). Also, advertisers are more likely to get a better mix of programs and to ensure they get their spots in the time periods and/or shows they want. The disadvantage, from the buyers' standpoint, is that there may be less room for negotiation because everyone is trying to buy from a limited

---

[1]"How the TV Nets Got the Upfront," Erwin Epron, *Ad Age Special Report on TV's Upfront*, May 14, 2001, p. S2/22; *Advertising Age*, June 20, 2005.

amount of inventory. That is, the networks can choose how much of the available airtime they wish to sell up front, manipulating the demand for that time. The buyers also don't know how well the new programs will perform, basing their judgment on brief promotional excerpts the networks release, along with their historical experience of similar shows from the past.

The commercial minutes the networks hold back or don't sell then form the bulk of the second type of national television time, which is known as the *scatter market* because it is scattered throughout the broadcast day across months. Buyers typically purchase this type of commercial time on a quarterly basis, usually 2 to 3 months in advance of the quarter, unless demand is soft. Prices in scatter will vary, depending on the supply and demand, and what happens in scatter tends to impact the long-term, or upfront, marketplace too. In boom years when the economy is thriving, advertiser demand during the upfront period is high, but when a recession hits, advertisers are loathe to commit large funds in advance and so upfront deals tend to decrease while scatter buys rise.

Advertisers who purchase spots in the scatter market may or may not get guaranteed ratings, depending on the supply and demand. Those spots are usually purchased by advertisers who are unable or unwilling to commit to a schedule a year in advance. If demand for scatter time is high, the network can "close" a particular daypart on very short notice, pulling it out of sale and then repricing it for future buyers. Advertisers who do not move quickly enough may find themselves shut out of the daypart completely.

Finally, the third way to buy time in national television is the *opportunistic* buy. Here, the advertiser chooses to purchase at the last minute, picking up whatever remains available. The advantage here is that the rates are usually most favorable to the buyer because the network wants to sell that time. The obvious drawback, however, is that there is less choice and little or no flexibility in the deal. Spots can be purchased as late as the day before airtime. Several sports events are sold this way.

Deciding how to purchase TV time depends on many factors, not the least of which is the size of the advertising budget. The number of quarters in which the commercial is to run also plays a key role here, as does the type of programming mix desired. First and foremost, however, should be strategic considerations regarding the impact of the decision on the marketing, advertising, and media goals.

How Television Time Is Bought

The way the process of buying television time works is as follows. The buyer requests a package of programs from the seller (broadcast, syndication, or cable). The package may be based on costs or on ratings, but ultimately it is based on the goals of the plan. The sellers submit their inventory, and the buyer chooses the package that best meets the client's needs and negotiates the price. Instead of purchasing them immediately, however, buyers "go to hold," which means buyers are almost certain they will buy that time but have not fully committed to it yet. Both sides agree on how long that "hold" will last; generally, it is 3 to five days in the scatter market, and 4 to 8 weeks in the long-term market. After that period, the buyer will either purchase the time or drop out. Once the deal is finalized, however, the buyer effectively owns that time. If, later on, buyers want to get rid of the commercial time they bought, the network may try to sell it to a different advertiser, if the marketplace demand is strong. On the other hand, if for some reason the spot does not run as promised, the buyer is given the option of a comparable spot on the program schedule. This is known as a *make-good*. That might mean moving with a program to another day or time, if the network decides to reschedule it, or staying in the same daypart but switching programs. When programs do not achieve the audience rating that the network had guaranteed to the advertiser, the network will then provide, over the course of a year, *audience deficiency units* (ADUs). These no-charge units are provided in same or comparable programs to the advertiser.

All national television time is priced based on a 30-second spot. For advertisers wishing to buy more or less time than that, the rates are adjusted accordingly. Hence, a 60-second spot costs twice as much, and a 15-second spot is half the full rate. Negotiations are conducted based on costs-per-thousand (CPMs) for the target, defined in terms of age and sex. For example, it could be the CPM for reaching women from age 18 to 49 or adults from age 25 to 54.

Buying Time on Syndication and Cable

Buying national television time on syndication and cable is not that different from the broadcast network marketplace. That is, there are long-term, scatter, and opportunistic buys available in each television form. Additional considerations need to be given, however, to the individual buys. With syndication, for example, *coverage* is critical. Because syndicated programs are sold to individual stations in each market, they may not be seen in every market across the country. The buyer therefore has to know what percent of stations in the United States will air a given program. It may be as low as 60%, or as high as 99%. The day and/or time of airing will also vary by town or city, and although people do watch programs rather than dayparts, it may well make a difference to the effectiveness of a media schedule if you are trying to reach women from age 25 to 54 with "Oprah" and find that it airs at 9:00 a.m. in Chattanooga, Tennessee, but at 3:00 p.m. in Gary, Indiana. The audience delivery and composition could be quite different in those markets because of that airtime variation.

Syndicated programs are guaranteed, but the syndicator may overstate the ratings estimate. That means the buyer then has to be given make-goods, either in the form of bonus units or cash back. Although this may seem easy to resolve, the syndication marketplace has been like this since its inception, and despite a decline in ratings beginning in the late 1990s, the marketplace still operates this way. Many packaged goods advertisers still rely on syndication to reach their "average" American consumers.

Cable television also sells a good deal of its commercial time in advance, usually with guaranteed ratings. Cable is bought either by individual program or by daypart rotation. A few networks, such as Nick-at-Nite and Headline News, largely sell time this way because there is strong enough advertiser demand for their units that they do not need to sell individual programs. This might appear to be a big problem for advertisers, but it is less critical on certain cable networks, where the programming is "vertical," and advertisers know that their spot will most likely air, for example, between music videos on MTV or in classic sitcoms on Nick-at-Nite. Most others have moved to program-based buys, because they have worked to create brand images for themselves based on their well-known personalities or, increasingly, their original programming. Examples here include Comedy Central's "The Daily Show" and ESPN's "Sports Center."

LOCAL TV AND RADIO BUYS

The purchase of time on spot television and spot radio has both similarities and differences to the network process. Local television buyers usually buy time on shorter notice than for national television. They also have to deal with individual stations in each market, rather than buying a complete network, unless they make a buy across various stations that are linked together into an ad sales network. The planner provides the buyer with the details of the specifications, which include the marketing and media objectives, a demographic and psychographic description of the target, the desired dayparts and flights, the number of ratings points per market and/or time period, the total budget, and the mix of commercial lengths (15, 30, and 60 seconds).

Armed with this information, the buyer can then start negotiating with stations in those markets. Rather than discuss the cost of an individual spot or the cost per thousand used in national television buys, both of which will vary considerably by market, buyers typically negotiate the cost per rating point (CPP). That way, they ensure that the appropriate number of rating points are purchased, at or below the amount budgeted. The negotiating process is quite subtle. The buyer does not want the seller to know how much money is available (as the station would want to get all of it!), and the seller does not want the buyer to know how much inventory is available (as that would let buyers know how low a price they could get). The buyer will usually talk to all of the stations in the market that have programs or formats appropriate for the target in the desired daypart and ask each of them to submit prices. For some advertisers, price is the most important criterion, so the buyer looks to purchase "tonnage," that is, lots of media weight at the lowest price available. For others, the program or format is key; they may be willing to pay slightly more to get a closer fit between target and vehicle. It depends on the strategy outlined in the media plan.

Once buyers have received submissions from each station, they can then start negotiating to see if any of the sellers are willing to lower their price any further. Whereas this used to take several days, in today's competitive climate buyers are less likely to give the stations much time to come in with a lower bid, and will usually decide fairly quickly which stations to purchase. Having made that decision, the final prices and terms are agreed to and the buy is made.

In theory, local television and radio buys are fixed; that is, the time is bought on a given daypart and/or program (unless the buyer purchases "run-of-schedule," or ROS, which means that the station can air the spot at any time). In practice, however, stations may preempt a spot if another advertiser comes in who is willing to pay more for that time slot. If this happens, the first advertiser will usually request a make-good or compensation if the station airs their spot at a less favorable time.

While buying local radio is similar in many respects to buying television, there are two opportunities for advertisers that are commonly made available in the audio medium. The first is merchandising and promotions. This has become an extremely important consideration for many companies that use spot radio, particularly national advertisers. Local radio stations may be willing, as part of the deal, to run special contests for listeners or set up a remote site broadcast or hold a special event for the trade, for example. The Scion car dealership could offer a new car as the grand prize in an on-air contest; the afternoon music show could be aired from the dealer's showroom, or a cocktail reception for all new Scion owners could be held at the radio station one evening. Such promotions need to be negotiated as part of the buy, but they may add considerably to the efficiency of the purchase.

The second difference that local radio can offer advertisers is the chance for live commercials. In the earliest days of radio, all commercials were spoken live by announcers on-air. Today, that is only possible at the local market level. Some advertisers believe that having a local radio personality deliver the message adds greater authority and credibility to the product, giving it an implied endorsement. Although this is not in fact true (the station never officially endorses any individual brand), it can be beneficial for the advertiser. In addition, because relatively few commercials are presented this way anymore, it offers another way to stand out from the crowd.

THE GREAT OUTDOORS

Because outdoor billboards are bought on a market-by-market basis, the buying process is, in some ways, akin to local TV and radio buying. Here, instead of dealing with individual TV or radio stations (or rep firms that put stations together into a network), the media buyer must either deal with individual outdoor plant operators, or with networks of plants that are available through large outdoor companies such as Clear Channel or Viacom.

Negotiations for outdoor billboards focus on several key elements: size, location, showing, and cost/CPM. The first criterion to consider is the poster or panel size—from an 8-sheet to a painted bulletin. As explained in chapter 4, different boards are purchased for different timeframes, with posters typically being sold on a 30-day basis and bulletins sold in a much longer term deal, such as 6 months or one year.

Location is really the key as far as outdoor is concerned. For certain products, such as a local restaurant, you might want to be on smaller posters in the city to remind people of your address; for hotels or gas stations, putting ads along highways to reach drivers as they are passing through your area would make more sense. And today, many advertisers place their billboards strategically close to their competitors' locations. CVS, for example, looks for boards that are near its key competitor, Walgreen's, reminding consumers as they get close to Walgreen's why they might want to reconsider that decision.

It is important, too, to know on which side of the street the board is located and whether there are any potential blockages that could get in the line of sight for the board, such as a tall building or tree. This kind of information can best be gained by actually going to the location to look at the board. The operator can provide you with a complete inventory of addresses for both bulletins and poster panels. In the case of posters, you can also find out if the poster is in an ethnic neighborhood and/or restricted location (no alcohol), and whether it is on a wall or a pole.

The outdoor showing that you buy will tell you what the number of daily exposures are to your message as a percentage of the total market size. A #100 showing, therefore, means that 100% of the audience will pass that board in a 30-day period; a #50 means 50% will do so, and so on. Showings are calculated based on traffic patterns, however, which means that not everyone who physically goes by the location will necessarily see your ad (just as a TV program rating does not mean the viewer will watch your commercial). Poster panels are generally bought at the 25, 50, or 100 showing level, whereas bulletins are purchased at 5, 10, or 15 showing increments. Each showing size in a market will have associated with it the number of poster panels utilized. This is known as the *allotment*.

Last, but not least, comes the cost of the buy. Outdoor is bought and sold on the basis of the cost of reaching 1,000 of the target audience, or CPM.

Unlike TV or radio, however, there are usually only a couple of operators to choose from in a given market, which limits the flexibility that the buyer has to negotiate. With considerable industry consolidation in recent years, many markets are now dominated by a single outdoor company that is part of a multimedia conglomerate. Even where there is more than one company to choose from, one will typically have better locations for a particular size board, whereas the other will have better offerings in a different size or location.

Once all of the negotiations have taken place, the media specialist will issue an outdoor authorization, laying out all of the details, or specifications, of the buy. These are then confirmed with the client and the seller, and the purchase can proceed.

IMPLEMENTING AN INTERNET BUY

Given the relative newness of the Internet as an advertising medium, the buying process for it continues to evolve. As with most other media forms, media specialists have the choice of working directly with individual Web sites, or placing buys with networks of aggregated sites, such as advertising.com. In either case, the media buyer negotiates the ad placement (fixed position or rotation) and cost, along with any special considerations, such as affiliate marketing or opt-in e-mails. *Affiliate marketing* involves a deal with the Web site whereby sales generated from a user who reached the sales site from your Web site receives a percentage of the revenue. *Opt-in e-mails* involve soliciting consumers to sign themselves up for e-mails from marketers based on the individual's declared interests. A newer type of buy is based on *behavioral* targeting, which targets users based on their prior behavior. For example, if you visit Amazon.com on a regular basis to look at the latest DVDs on sale, then you might be sent an ad from a Hollywood studio or Blockbuster, because your behavior indicates you have an interest in movies. The benefit for advertisers is that they can find their target audience in places where they might not have expected them to be. Companies such as Revenue Science and Tacoda work heavily in this area. The overall goal of these approaches is to find sites that the target considers *contextually relevant*. This may mean relevance to the campaign, such as an ad for Kellogg's Special K cereal that touts its value in a dieting plan on e-diets.com. Or, it can be relevance to the target's mind-set, such as ads that include JD Power award rankings appearing when a user is clicking on an automotive Web site searching for new car information.

In addition, the buyer has to determine with the seller the basis for the sale—cost per thousand impressions, cost per click, or cost per transaction, for example. Research of those who come to the site is often included as a "value added" bonus, although the drawback here is that it could be biased in favor of the site if they are conducting or hosting the survey. An alternative is to pay for "neutral" third-party research through companies such as Dynamic Logic and Insight Express. In either case, the idea is to sample every n-th person who comes to the site and offer that person a survey that can include questions about advertising recognition or brand attitudes.

BUYING NONTRADITIONAL MEDIA

For advertisers looking to create an integrated marketing plan, the buys may be as varied as the media elements themselves. Sponsorships, for example, are usually sold by the venue (sports stadium, concert stadium). Direct mail is purchased by buying mailing lists and working through a mailing house to execute the campaign. Brand integration into TV shows and movies is currently offered by the producers of the entertainment, although some believe that in the case of television, the networks themselves will want to enter into this highly profitable arena, especially as they lose revenues from traditional commercial sales. And for public relations or viral marketing, there is likely to be no official "buy" made at all. There may be some out-of-pocket costs (e.g., creation of a video news release to send to TV stations, or payment of the people who are "planted" in a social scene to promote your product). Whichever the method used to make the nontraditional buy, it is the media specialist's job to negotiate the price (wherever possible), and determine the metrics against which the cost of the program will be evaluated (traffic, impressions, clicks, etc). The goal should be to try to make these buys as comparable as possible to the other media in the plan.

SUMMARY

Even the most impressive media plan will not achieve its goals if the buys are not made effectively. That means the time and space need to be purchased in accordance with the plan's specifications, in terms of criteria such as timing, ad size, and placement or position within the media vehicle. For magazines and newspapers, editorial adjacencies may be key, so that the ad message is seen in an appropriate context, such as an ad for Verizon cellular phone service targeting business people in the Business section of the *Wall Street Journal* or an Olay antiwrinkle cream targeting women in the Beauty section of *Marie Claire* magazine. The costs for print media may be negotiable, off the rate card, depending on the competitiveness of the magazine category.

Buying time on electronic media is always done through negotiations, either with a network or individual stations. TV buys may be long term (purchased upfront) or short term (in the scatter market). The guarantees and costs of those buys will vary accordingly. For radio, where most time is purchased locally, buyers deal with stations or rep firms that sell them a package of stations across the markets in which the buyer is interested. Deals are usually made based on the cost per rating point. For outdoor billboards, the key buying criterion to consider is the location of the board, whether a poster or a bulletin. Buyers negotiate the cost to reach a given proportion of the market, estimated using showings. The process can be handled with individual plant operators or through networks. For the Internet, the buys are made with individual sites or networks that aggregate those sites. The buys are based on placement, rotation, and metrics. With nontraditional media, it is the specialist's job to negotiate fair market value and determine the metrics against which to evaluate the media impact.

CHECKLIST—MAKING THE MEDIA BUYS

1. Do you have all the necessary specifications regarding the objectives, the target audience, vehicle preferences, GRP needs, and budget limitations to proceed to the buys?
2. Does the client have to approve the buys before they are finalized?
3. For magazines, is a discount available for a volume buy?
4. Do you want a preferred position for your magazine ad?
5. Are you trying to reach a more specialized or generalized audience with magazines (priced accordingly)?
6. Are any special promotions, editorial features, bonus circulation, or trade deals being offered by any of the magazines?
7. Do you want your newspaper ad to appear in a special section?
8. Are there any special instructions needed for your newspaper ad, such as a coupon or inclusion of color?
9. Do you want to buy time on network, cable, or syndicated TV?
10. Is your national television buy going to be made for the long term (up-front) or short term (scatter)?
11. Can you get ratings guarantees for your national TV buy?
12. For a syndicated TV buy, what is your clearance?
13. With a cable TV buy, do you want a specific time period or will a rotation suffice?
14. For a local TV buy, is media weight (tonnage) more important than specific program selection?
15. For local radio or local TV, do you want to deal directly with each station, or do you prefer to use a rep firm?
16. Are your outdoor billboards' locations satisfactory?
17. Do you have enough billboards in each market to generate sufficient showings?
18. Have you negotiated ad placement and type with individual Web sites, search engines, or networks?

19. What are the terms of negotiation for your nontraditional media?
20. What are the metrics you are using for the nontraditional media against which you will evaluate its cost efficiency and impact?

CHAPTER 9

Evaluating the Media Plan

One of the most often-repeated quotations about advertising was attributed to John Wanamaker, Philadelphia department store magnate, who said that he knew half of the money he spent on advertising was wasted; he just didn't know which half. Your job, as a media specialist, is to try to ensure that your client's dollars are not wasted. One way to achieve that is by evaluating the media plan before it is executed, and then again once it is up and running.

It is no longer true that an annual plan is left unchanged for a whole year; it is more common for advertisers to make changes to at least some part of the marketing plan while the campaign is running. This may be in response to changes in any part of the marketing mix. Consumer response could end up being greater or less than anticipated; product improvements could necessitate additional promotional efforts; new channels of distribution could become important; or competitive pricing strategies may require alterations to the original, approved plan. And, beyond that, economic trends can affect almost all marketing efforts. For example, in recessionary times, most "experts" tend to predict that the economic hard times will be over soon, suggesting that consumer spending will improve. What often happens is that consumer confidence in the economy remains low for longer than such optimistic forecasts, leading people to continue their restrained purchasing habits. This has a marked effect on the manufacturers of high-ticket items such as cars and electronics. It also impacts general eating habits, causing people to eat out less and stay home more.

This chapter presents four of the ways that a media plan can be evaluated, before and after it begins running. We have explained the concepts of reach and frequency. With today's sophisticated computer tools, syndicated data on past purchase and media consumption can be analyzed to give a "best guess" estimate of how well a medium, or total plan, will reach the chosen target audience. This can later be compared with actual results on reach and frequency, to see how well the plan actually performed, which is crucial information for preparing next year's plan. The second type of evaluation is to check that your ads actually run as scheduled, a practice known as post-buy analysis. It is up to the media specialist to make sure that if, for some reason, the ad did not run as scheduled or was not positioned in the agreed-on place, that some form of compensation is given, either monetary or in time or space. Thirdly, it may well be worthwhile spending additional dollars to research the consumer impact of the media (and/or marketing) plan. After you doubled the spending levels in television, are your brand's awareness levels considerably higher? How well is your commercial message being recalled now that you have switched dollars out of magazines and into radio? These kinds of questions can best be answered by talking to some of the consumers you were trying to reach. Last but not least, in the weeks and months after your plan is executed, you can hire econometricians to assess the return on investment, or payout, of your plan.

PRE-PLAN ANALYSIS

The first time to evaluate the impact of the media plan is before it is presented to the client. That is, in selecting the media vehicles you think will best meet the advertising and marketing objectives, the media specialist needs to figure out which combination of vehicles will do the best job of reaching the target an acceptable number of times. Computer systems and tools are readily available to help make these kinds of analyses simple and fast.

For example, let's say you were considering two alternative combinations for your media plan for Pillsbury cake mix. The first combination would use monthly insertions in *Redbook* magazine, along with periodic commercials in prime time on the Lifetime cable television network. Another possibility would be to place continuous messages on cable, with occasional ads in the magazine. Here is how the two schedules might look for the year:

TABLE 9.1

Schedule 1	Schedule 2
10 insertions in Redbook	4 insertions in Redbook
(50 GRPs)	(20 GRPs)
400 GRPs in Lifetime	1,000 GRPs in Lifetime

And here is how the two schedules would perform against your target of women from age 25 to 54:

TABLE 9.2

	Schedule 1	Schedule 2
Total GRPs	450	1,020
Reach 1+	34.1 %	32.6%
Reach 3+	25.2%	22.7%
Frequency	13.2	31.3

So, even though you are using far more cable in Schedule 2, the impact on the overall reach is actually less than if you used more magazine advertising, as in Schedule 1.

POST-BUY ANALYSIS

What the media specialist must find out once the plan is running is whether the ads ran as scheduled, and how well the plan actually delivered. For the first part, determining that the ads did in fact run as scheduled, you can turn to various sources, depending on the medium. For newspapers, there are *tear sheets*, which are provided by commercial services, to show you examples of the actual ad in the newspaper. Magazines will usually provide copies of the issues in which your ad appears. For television and radio, you should receive affidavits confirming when your spot aired. And, increasingly, as the buys become wholly electronic, advertising agencies are starting to be able to monitor 'ad executions within hours or days of their airing (rather than the weeks or months it used to take). With the Internet, you can easily go online to make sure your ad appears, or use a third-party service to verify its location and rotation. In each case, the media specialist must check that the terms of the contract were adhered to. If you requested being in the food section of the paper, or the first third of the magazine, is that where your ad was placed?

For broadcast media, the task is usually more complicated because program schedules are far more prone to being changed. You might have arranged for your radio spot to air between 6:00 p.m. and 8:00 p.m., only to find that it came on at 5:30 p.m. or 8:20 p.m. Or, you could have bought a rotation of spots (ROS, or run of schedule), which in theory means that your spots will run equitably in all dayparts. In analyzing the affidavits or electronic reports you might discover that more than one half of the messages were aired between midnight and 6:00 a.m., or some other inappropriate time. It is then incumbent on the station to explain what happened and, in all likelihood, offer some type of make-good, either in the form of free ads or financial compensation for the cost differences between ROS and the overnight period.

In larger agencies or organizations, this postanalysis checking is typically done by the media buyers or business service department. It is more of an accounting than a media function, but ultimately, the media specialist should know what happened, and why.

Later on, additional information becomes available to show how your ad schedule delivered. This is in the form of syndicated data, such as Nielsen for television, Arbitron for radio, Mediamark Research, Inc. (MRI) for print media, and Nielsen NetRatings for the Web. Each service provides the ratings and audience delivery of media vehicles to help you determine whether, in fact, you met the goals of your plan. Other companies can access this data also, acting as third-party vendors of the information.

The kinds of questions the data can help you answer include what percentage of the target was reached by the media (and vehicles) that you used (reach), and how often, on average, was the target exposed to them? It is worth emphasizing again that these terms refer only to media exposure, and not to actual exposure to the ads themselves. They should therefore be thought of as *opportunities to see* your message. Many advertisers will discount, or "weight," the exposure levels to account for this distinction, assuming, for example, that only half of the people reached by the media vehicle will actually see the ad. Or, they may only look at the proportion of the target that is exposed a certain number of times (*effective reach*), assuming here that people will require several opportunities to see your message before they in fact will do so.

CUSTOM CONSUMER RESEARCH

The importance of evaluating the plan's impact on consumers once it has gone into effect cannot be underestimated. By doing so you will find out, first, whether you got what you (or your client) paid for, and second, whether or not the plan worked as you intended. It will provide invaluable help in preparing for next year's plan too. This may be by undertaking surveys of consumers before and after their exposure to your ads, to assess their brand recall and any brand attitude shifts. Or, it could be through qualitative research, such as focus groups or in-depth interviews, where consumers are asked to explain their feelings about their media exposure in greater detail. Why did they pay attention to the TV ads but ignore the radio ads, for example? How were the Internet ads effective (or not) in influencing their purchase decision? Although, ultimately, the impact of the media plan, and the other elements of the marketing mix, is determined at the cash register, it is helpful to be able to analyze the individual parts to find out what is, or is not, working. Having said that, and acknowledging the truth to this chapter's opening comment by John Wanamaker, you should keep in mind that it is difficult to determine the precise effect of advertising media messages on consumers. We know *when* it is working, but we may not always know *how*.

ROI IMPACT

For more sophisticated analyses of media's impact, *econometric modeling* can provide the answer. Here, as noted in chapter 6, complex statistical models analyze as many of the marketing mix variables as possible (depending on the category) to see what role advertising media play in generating sales (or other goals, e.g., awareness, consideration, or purchase intent). The models can look at everything from GRPs to distribution to weather patterns, and attempt to isolate the part that each plays in the mix.

Without evaluating how a media plan performs, we are left even more in the dark than when we began. In effect, it means that each time we create a plan, we end up recreating the wheel. This can lead you down two paths. Either the same plan is reproduced because it "seemed to work" (or at least, didn't cause any disasters). Or, the plan is completely changed to see if that makes a difference in sales, awareness, or attitudes. Both of these options are flawed. To continue doing exactly the same thing as before without knowing whether it is working, or if it could possibly be improved, is detrimental to your product and client, keeping them from performing at their best. Similarly, to overturn the plan without analyzing how it worked (or didn't work) means that you run the risk of losing the momentum your ads might have started to build, and jeopardizes your chances for success.

So although there is a strong temptation, once the media plan is completed and the ads are running, to file it away and move on to the next stage, true media specialists will carry on the task through to the end. They are responsible for ensuring not only that the ads run as intended, but that they have delivered what was planned. If these two evaluation tasks are carried out successfully, then you will have a more satisfied client and you will have already taken an important step forward in preparing for next year's media plan.

SUMMARY

A completed media plan is really not final until it has been evaluated to see how it has performed. This should be done both before the plan is executed, by calculating estimates of reach and frequency that the plan should achieve, and afterward, through post-buy analyses to ensure that the ads ran as scheduled. If the messages did not air as intended and specified in the buys, then it is up to the media specialist to obtain some type of compensation. Consumer research and ROI analysis can provide further evidence of how well the plan delivered. Without these checks, there is no way of knowing whether this year's plan should be continued into the following year with or without modifications. And, although it is always difficult to pinpoint precisely the impact of advertising on sales, the process of evaluating the success or failure of the media plan in achieving the media, advertising, and marketing objectives will help the brand and the client know how to do better next year.

CHECKLIST—EVALUATING THE MEDIA PLAN

1. Have you performed reach and frequency analyses of the media plan before presenting it to the client?
2. Have you contacted clipping services or the print media themselves to determine that your ads ran as scheduled?
3. Are the post-buys for electronic media available to ensure that your ads ran as scheduled?
4. Do you have access to syndicated data (e.g., Nielsen, Arbitron, MRI, and SMRB) for future analysis of how your media vehicles performed against your target?
5. Do you have a plan in place to conduct consumer research to understand how or whether the plan worked?
6. Are you able to perform ROI analysis of the plan's impact on sales?
7. Do you have ideas on how your media plan can be improved for next year?

Appendix A: Key Research Resources

Advertising Age
711 Third Avenue
New York, NY 10017-4036
(212) 210–0100
www.adage.com
Industry trade journal, published weekly.

Advertising Research Foundation
641 Lexington Avenue
New York, NY 10022
(212) 751–5656
www.arfsite.org
Industry research organization.

Adweek
770 Broadway, 7th Floor
New York, NY 10003
(646) 654–5117
www.adweek.com
Industry trade journal, published weekly.

Arbitron
142 West 57th Street
New York, NY 10019-3300
(212) 887–1300
www.arbitron.com
Radio audience measurement company, using weekly listening diaries
and testing personal portable meters (PPM).

Audit Bureau of Circulations
900 N. Meacham Road
Schaumburg, IL 60173
(847) 605–0909
www.accessabc.com
Circulation auditing company for magazine and newspaper industry.

Claritas
5375 Mira Sorrento Place, Suite 400
San Diego, CA 92121
(800) 866–6520
www.claritas.com
Company offers computerized mapping system to display consumer, media, and lifestyle traits by geography.

TNS Media Intelligence (formerly CMR)
100 Park Avenue, 4th Floor
New York, NY 10017
(212) 991–6000
www.tns-mi.com
Measures advertisers' media spending across 20 media types.

Donovan Data Systems
115 West 18th Street
New York, NY 10011
(212) 633–8100
www.donovandata.com
Third-party processor of Nielsen TV audience data; also, major bill payment system for advertising agencies.

Information Resources Inc.
150 N Clinton Street
Chicago, IL 60661-1416
(312) 726–1221
www.infores.com
Collects and reports consumer package goods, sales using supermarket checkout data.

Interactive Market Systems
770 Broadway, 15th Floor
New York, NY 10003
(646) 654–5900
www.imsms.com
Third-party media software company that provides media planning tools to assess multimedia audiences.

Intermedia Advertising Group
345 Park Avenue
New York, NY 10013
(212) 871–5200
www.iagr.net
Company measures audience ad recall and ad likability of prime-time TV ads via consumer web panel, Reward TV.

JD Power & Associates
2625 Townsgate Road, Suite 100

Westlake Village, CA 91361
(805) 418–8000
www.jdpa.com
Provides annual demographic, lifestyle, and media information linked
to automotive industry.

Kantar Media Research
230 Park Avenue South, 5th Floor
New York, NY 10003
(212) 548–7250
www.kmrgroup.com
Parent company to several audience research companies (TGI), as well as
software provider of media optimization systems (X-Pert, Supermidas).
Owned by WPP.

Mediamark Research, Inc.
75 Ninth Avenue
New York, NY 10011
(212) 884–9200
www.mediamark.com
Measures demographic, media, and lifestyle information among 40,000
adults per year. Used for target and audience analysis.

Monroe Mendelsohn Research
841 Broadway
New York, NY 10003-4704
(212) 677–8100
www.mmrsurverys.com
Provides media, demographic, and lifestyle information for upper-in-
come adults.

Nielsen Media Research
770 Broadway
New York, NY 10003
(646) 654–8300
www.nielsenmedia.com
Main provider of national and local television viewing information. National service based on national panel of 10,000 adults using people meters; local service based on local people meters in top 10 markets by
2006; household set meters (top 55 markets), and additional weekly
viewing diaries (all remaining non-LPM markets).

Scarborough Research
770 Broadway
New York, NY 10003
(646) 654–8400
www.scarborough.com
Measures demographic, media, and lifestyle information in 75 local
markets.

Simmons
230 Park Avenue South, 5th Floor
New York, NY 10003-1566
(212) 598–5400
www.smrb.com
Collects demographic, media, and lifestyle information on 40,000 adults
each year. Also offers special annual studies on children, teens, and Hispanics.

Spectra Marketing
200 West Jackson, Suite 2800
Chicago, IL 60606-6910
(312) 583–5100
www.spectramarketing.com
Marketing analysis.

Standard Rate & Data Service
1700 Higgins Road
Des Plaines, IL 60018-5605
(847) 375–5000
www.srds.com
Provides databases of media rates and information on all major media
categories.

Telmar Information Services
470 Park Avenue South, 15th Floor
New York, NY 10016
(212) 725–3000
www.telmar.com
Third-party media software company that provides media planning
tools to assess multimedia audiences.

Yankelovich Partners
400 Meadowmont Village Circle, Suite 431
Chapel Hill, NC 27517
(919) 932–8600
www.yankelovich.com
Consumer research company that offers annual trend studies on various
demographic or lifestyle segments.

Appendix B: Key Media Organizations

Advertising Council
261 Madison Avenue, 11th Floor
New York, NY 10016
(212) 922–1500
www.adcouncil.org
Organization sponsoring and promoting public service advertising.

Advertising Club of New York
235 Park Avenue South, 6th Floor
New York, NY 10003
(212) 522–8080
www.theadvertisingclub.org
Forum for ad professionals.

Advertising Educational Foundation
220 East 42nd Street, Suite 3300
New York, NY 10017
(212) 986–8060
www.aef.com
Distributes educational content to enrich understanding of advertising.

Advertising Research Foundation
641 Lexington Avenue
New York, NY 10022
(212) 751–5656
Industry organization focused on Advertising and Media Research.

Advertising Women of New York
25 West 45th Street, Suite 1001
(212) 221–7969
www.awny.org
Forum to advance women in the field of communications.

American Association of Advertising Agencies (AAAA)
405 Lexington Avenue
New York, NY 10174
(212) 682–2500
www.aaaa.org

Main trade organization of advertising agencies.

American Advertising Federation (AAF)
1101 Vermont Avenue NW, Suite 500
Washington, DC 20005
(202) 898–0089
www.aaf.org
Protects and promotes advertising. Sponsors annual National Student
Ad Competition (NSAC) and has 210 college chapters with 6,800 under-
graduate members. Offers 1,000+ internship opportunities.

American Business Media
675 Third Avenue
New York, NY 10017
(212) 661–6360
www.americanbusinessmedia.com
Association for business-to-business information providers.

American Marketing Association
311 South Wacker Drive, Suite 5800
Chicago, IL 60606
(312) 542–9000
www.marketingpower.org
Professional association for marketers.

Art Directors Club
106 West 29th Street
New York, NY 10001
(212) 643–1440
www.adcglobal.org
International group focused on the creative product.

Association of Hispanic Advertising Agencies
8201 Greensboro Drive, 3rd Floor
Mclean, VA 22102
(703) 610–9014
www.ahaa.org
Trade group for Hispanic advertising agencies

Association of National Advertisers (ANA)
708 Third Avenue
New York, NY 10017
(212) 697–5950
www.ana.net
Main trade organization for national advertisers.

Cabletelevision Advertising Bureau (CAB)
830 Third Avenue
New York, NY 10022
(212) 508–1200

www.onetvworld.org
Trade organization for the cable TV industry.

Direct Marketing Association (DMA)
1120 Avenue of the Americas
New York, NY 10036
(212) 768–7277
www.the-dma.org
Trade organization for the direct marketing industry.

Interactive Advertising Bureau (IAB)
116 East 27th Street
New York, NY 10016
(212) 380–4700
www.iab.net
Trade group promoting interactive advertising on the Web.

International Advertising Association (IAA)
521 Fifth Avenue, Suite 1807
New York, NY 10175
(212) 557–1133
www.iaaglobal.org
Professional group focused on advertising as a global industry. Has chapters in several U.S. universities.

Magazine Publishers of America
810 Seventh Avenue
New York, NY 10022
(212) 872–3700
www.magazine.org
Trade group promoting magazines.

National Advertising Review Council
70 West 36th Street, 13th Floor
New York, NY 10018
(866) 334 NARC (6272)
www.narcpartners.org
Provides guidelines and sets standards of truth and accuracy for national advertisers.

National Assocation of Broadcasters (NAB)
1771 N Street NW
Washington, DC 20036
(202) 429–5300
www.nab.org
Trade group promoting the broadcast television industry.

Newspaper Association of America (NAA)
1921 Gallows Road, Suite 600
Vienna, VA 22182

(703) 902–1600
www.naa.org
Trade group promoting newspapers.

The One Club
21 East 26th Street, 5th Floor
New York, NY 10010
(212) 979–1900
www.oneclub.org
Organization to promote excellence in advertising through an annual
creative awards show.

Online Publishers Association (OPA)
500 Seventh Avenue, 14th Floor
New York, NY 10018
(212) 600–6342
www.online-publishers.org
Trade group for online content providers.

Outdoor Advertising Association of America (OAAA)
1850 M Street NW, Suite 1040
Washington, DC 20036
(212) 833–5566
www.oaaa.org
Trade group promoting the outdoor advertising industry.

Point of Purchase Advertising Institute (POPAI)
1660 L Street NW
Washington, DC 20036
(202) 530–3000
www.popai.org
Trade group promoting the "marketing at-retail" industry.

Promotion Marketing Association (PMA)
257 Park Avenue South, 11th Floor
New York, NY 10010
(212) 420–1100
www.pmalink.org
The voice of the promotion industry.

Radio Advertising Bureau (RAB)
1320 Greenway drive, Suite 500
Irving, TX 75038
(800) 232–3131
www.rab.com
Trade group promoting radio advertising.

Syndicated Network Television Association (SNTA)
630 Fifth Avenue, Suite 2320
New York, NY 10011

(212) 259–3740
www.snta.org
Trade group promoting television syndication.

Television Bureau of Advertising (TVB)
3 East 54th Street, 10th Floor
New York, NY 10022
(212) 486–1111
www.tvb.org
Trade group promoting the broadcast television industry, with particular focus on spot TV.

Traffic Bureau of Advertising for Media Measurement (TBA)
420 Lexington Avenue, Suite 2520
New York, NY 10170
(212) 972–8075
www.tabonline.com
Audits circulation of out of home media and supports other out of home research initiatives.

Word of Mouth Marketing Association (WOMMA)
333 West North Avenue, #500
Chicago, IL 60610
(312) 335–0035
Trade association for the word of mouth marketing industry.

Yellow Pages Integrated Media Association
Two Connell Drive, 1st Floor
Berkeley Heights, NJ 07922
(908) 286–2380
www.ypima.org
Trade group promoting yellow pages marketing, both in print and online.

References

Abernathy, Avery M. "The Information Content of Newspaper Advertising," Journal of Current Issues and Research in Advertising, vol. 14, no. 2, Fall 1992, 63-68.

Abernathy, Avery M. "Advertising Clearance Practices of Radio Stations: A Model of Advertising Self-Regulation," Journal of Advertising, vol. 22, no. 3, September 1993, 13-26.

Abernathy, Avery M., and David N. Laband. "The Customer Pulling Power of Different Sized Yellow Pages Advertising," Journal of Advertising Research, vol. 42, no. 3, May/June 2002, 66-72.

Appel, Valentine. "Editorial Environment and Advertising Effectiveness," Journal of Advertising Research, vol. 27, no. 4, August/September 1987, 11-16

Atkinson, Claire. "DVRs: A $27B Revenue Killer," Advertising Age, April 18. 2005, 45

Aylesworth, Andrew B. and Scott B. MacKenzie. "Context is Key: The Effect of Program-Induced Mood on Thoughts About the Ad," Journal of Advertising, vol. 27, no. 2, Summer 1998, 17-32.

Baltas, George. "Determinants of Internet Advertising: An Empirical Study," International Journal of Market Research, vol. 45, no. 4, 505-513.

Bhargava, Mukesh, Naveen Donthu, and Rosanne Caron. "Improving the Effectiveness of Outdoor Advertising: Lessons from a Study of 282 Campaigns," Journal of Advertising Research, vol. 34, no. 2, March/April 1994, 46-55.

Broach Jr, V. Carter, Thomas R. Page, Jr, and R. Dale Wilson. "Television Programming and Its Influence on Viewers' Perceptions of Commercials: The Role of Program Arousal and Pleasantness," Journal of Advertising, vol. 24, no. 4, Winter 1995, 45-54.

Briggs, Rex. "How the Internet is Reshaping Advertising," Admap, Issue 560, April 2005, 59-61.

Bryce, Wendy J. and Richard F. Yalch. "Hearing Versus Seeing: A Comparison of Consumer Learning of Spoken and Pictorial Information in Television Advertising," Journal of Current Issues and Research in Advertising, vol. 15, no. 1, Spring 1993, 1-20.

Buchholz, Laura M. and Robert E. Smith. "The Role of Consumer Involvement in Determining Cognitive Response to Broadcast Advertising," Journal of Advertising, vol. 20, no. 1 1991, 4-17.

Cannon, Hugh M. and Edward A. Riordan. "Effective Reach and Frequency: Does It Really Make Sense?", Journal of Advertising Research, vol. 34, no. 2, March/April 1994, 19-28.

Dobson, Chris. "Changing Fortunes for Internet Advertising," Admap, Issue 448, March 2004, 32-33.

Edwards, Steven and Carrie La Ferle. "Cross Media Promotion of the Internet in Television Commercials," Journal of Current Issues and Research in Advertising, vol. 22, no. 1, Spring 2000, 1-12.

Elliott , Michael T. and Paul Surgi Speck. "Consumer Perceptions of Advertising Clutter and Its Impact Across Various Media," Journal of Advertising Research, vol. 35, no. 3, May/June 1995, 29-42.

Ephron, Erwin. "More Weeks, Less Weight: The Shelf Space Model of Advertising," Journal of Advertising Research, vol. 35, no. 3, May/June 1995, 18-24.

Ephron, Erwin. "Recency Planning,"Journal of Advertising Research, vol. 37, no. 4, July/August 1997, 61-65.

Ephron, Erwin. "Point of View: Optimizers and Media Planning," Journal of Advertising Research, vol. 38, no. 4, July/August 1998, 47-56.

Ephron, Erwin. "How the TV Nets Got the Upfront," Ad Age Special Report on TV's Upfront, May 14, 2001, p S2/22, Advertising Age, June 20, 2005.

Fernandez, Karen V. and Dennis L. Rosen. "The Effectiveness of Information and Color in Yellow Pages Advertising," Journal of Advertising, vol. 29, no. 2, Summer 2000, 59-72.

Gibson, Lawrence D. "What Can One Exposure Do?", Journal of Advertising Research, vol. 36, no. 1, March/April 1996, 9-18.

Ha, Louisa, and Barry R. Litman. "Does Advertising Clutter Have Diminishing and Negative Returns?" Journal of Advertising, vol. 26, no. 1, Spring 1997, 31-42.

Halliday, Jean, and Claire Atkinson. "Pontiac Gets Major Mileage Out of $8 Million 'Oprah' Deal," Advertising Age, September 20, 2004, 12.

Homer, Pamela M. "Ad Size as an Indicator of Perceived Advertising Costs and Effort: The Effects on Memory and Perceptions," Journal of Advertising, vol. 24, no. 4, Winter 1995, 1-12.

Johannes, Amy. "Burger King Cooks Up a Winner: Best Overall," Promo Magazine Website, May 3, 2005.

Jones, John Philip. When Ads Work, Lexington Books, 1995.

Jones, John Philip. "Single Source Research Begins to Fulfill Its Promise," Journal of Advertising Research, vol. 35, no. 3, May/June 1995, 9-17.

Jones, John Philip. The Ultimate Secrets of Advertising, Sage Publications, 2002.

Kamins, Michael A., Lawrence J. Marks, and Deborah Skinner. "Television Commercial Evaluation in the Context of Program Induced Mood: Congruency Versus Consistency Effects," Journal of Advertising, vol. 20, no. 2, June 1991, 1-14.

Klaussen, Abbey. "More NBC Affiliates Drop 'Book of Daniel'," AdAge.com, January 12, 2006.

Ko, Hanjun, Chung-Hoan Cho, and Marilyn S. Robinson. "Internet Uses and Gratifications," Journal of Advertising, vol. 34, no. 2, Summer 2005, 57-70.

Krugman, Dean M., Glen T. Cameron, and Candace McKearney-White. "Visual Attention to Programming and Commercials: The Use of In-Home Observations," Journal of Advertising, vol. 24, no. 1, Spring 1995, 1-12.

Krugman, Herbert E. "Memory Without Recall, Exposure Without Perception," Journal of Advertising Research, vol. 40, no 6, November/December 2000, 49-54.

Kubas Consultants. "Reenergizing Readership and Revitalizing Newspapers," Presented at Newspaper Association of America conference, November 2003.

Leigh, James H. "Information Processing Differences Among Broadcast Media: Review and Suggestions for Research," Journal of Advertising, vol. 20, no. 2, June 1991, 71-76.

Longman, Kenneth A. "If Not Effective Frequency, Then What?", Journal of Advertising Research, vol. 37, no.4, July/August 1997, 44-50.

Lord, Kenneth R. and Robert E. Burnkrant. "Attention Versus Distraction: The Interactive Effect of Program Involvement and Attentional Devices on Commercial Processing," Journal of Advertising, vol. 22, no. 1, March 1993, 47-60.

Lord, Kenneth R. and Sanjay Putrevu. "Communicating in Print: A Comparison of Consumer Responses to Different Promotional Formats," Journal of Current Issues and Research in Advertising, vol. 20, no. 2, Fall 1998, 1-18.

MacArthur, Kate. "McSwindle," Ad Age, August 27, 2001, p 1/pp 22-23.

MacArthur, Kate. "Pepsi Smash TV Show Moves to Yahoo," AdAge.com, June 3, 2005.

Magazine Publishers of America (MPA) Website at www.magazine.org for more information on Millward Brown study of ad effectiveness, the AC Nielsen Sales Scan study, and econometric modeling case analysis, Measuring the Mix.

Michaels, Burt. "Putting a 21st Century Spin on a Powerful Selling Vehicle," Know Magazine, p51-58.

Miller, Darryl W. and Lawrence J. Marks. "Mental Imagery and Sound Effects in Radio Commercials," Journal of Advertising, vol. 21, no. 4, December 1992, 83-94.

Moore, Robert S., Claire Allison Stammerjohan, and Robin A. Coulter. "Banner Advertiser-Web Site Context Congruity and Color Effects on Attention and Attitudes," Journal of Advertising, vol. 34, no. 2, Summer 2005, 71-84.

Moya Schilling, Maria Christina, Karin Wood, and Alan Branthwaite. "The Medium is Part of the Message," ESOMAR, Reinventing Advertising, Rio, November 2000, 207-229.

Naples, Michael J. "Effective Frequency – Then and Now," Journal of Advertising Research, vol. 37, no. 4, July/August 1997, 7-13.

Norris, Claire E. and Andrew M. Colman. "Context Effects on Recall and Recognition of Magazine Advertisements," Journal of Advertising, vol. 21, no. 3, September 1992, 37-46.

Olsen, G. Douglas. "Creating the Contrast: The Influence of Silence and Background Music on Recall and Attribute Importance," Journal of Advertising, vol. 24, no. 4, Winter 1995, 29-44.

Online Publishers Association. "Online User Experience Study," 2005.

Osborne, Lawrence. "Consuming Rituals," New York Times Magazine, January 13, 2002, 28-31.

Radio Advertising Effectiveness Lab (RAEL) studies, 2004-2005 Radio Marketing Guide & Fact Book, produced by the Radio Advertising Bureau, New York.

Roper Starch Study, on behalf of Newspaper Association of America, 2001.

Sibley, Stanley D. and James C. Tsao. "Displacement and Reinforcement Effects of the Internet and Other Media as Sources of Information," Journal of Advertising Research, vol. 44, no. 1, March 2004, 126-142.

Smith, Robert E. and Laura M. Buchholz. "Multiple Resource Theory and Consumer Processing of Broadcast Advertisements: An Involvement Perspective," Journal of Advertising vol. 20, no. 3, September 1991, 1-8.

Srinivasan, Srini S., Robert P. Leone, and Francis J. Mulhern. "The Advertising Exposure Effect of Free-Standing Inserts," Journal of Advertising, vol. 24, no.1, Spring 1995, 29-40.

Stapel, Jan. "Recall and Recognition: A Very Close Relationship," Journal of Advertising Research, vol. 38, no. 4, July/August 1998, 41-46.

Surgi Speck, Paul, and Michael T. Elliott, "Predictors of Advertising Avoidance in Print and Broadcast Media," Journal of Advertising, vol. 26, no. 2, Summer 1997, 61-76.

Surgi Speck, Paul, and Michael T. Elliott. "The Antecedents and Consequences of Perceived Advertising Clutter," Journal of Current Issues and Research in Advertising, vol. 19, no. 2, 1997, 39-54.

Surgi Speck, Paul, and Michael T. Elliott. "Predictors of Advertising Avoidance in Print and Broadcast Media," Journal of Advertising, vol. 26, no. 2, Summer 1997, 61-76.

Tavassoli, Nader T., Clifford J. Shultz II, and Gavan J. Fitzsimons. "Program Involvement: Are Moderate Levels Best for Ad Memory and Attitude Toward the Ad?", Journal of Advertising Research, vol. 35, no. 5, September/October 1995, 61-72.

Taylor, Elizabeth Gigi, and Wei-Na Lee. "A Cross-Media Study of Audience Choice: The Influence of Media Attitudes on Individual Selection of Media Repertoires," Proceedings of the 2004 Conference of the American Academy of Advertising, 39-48.

Tellis, Gerard. "Effective Frequency: One Exposure or Three Factors?" Journal of Advertising Research, vol. 37, no. 4, July/August 1997, 75-80.

Tolley, Stuart. "A Study of National Advertising's Payout: Image Ads in Newspaper ROP," Journal of Advertising Research, vol. 33, no. 5, September/October 1993, 11-20.

Ware, Britta C. "Magazine Reader Involvement Improves ROI," ESOMAR, Print Audience Measurement, LA, June 2003.

Whitney, Daisy. "Sharing the Spotlight," New York Times, May 10, 2005, ZX11.

Yi, Youjae. "Contextual Priming Effects in Print Advertisements: The Moderating Role of Prior Knowledge," Journal of Advertising, vol. 22, no. 1, March 1993, 1-10.

Index